Flower A. Newhouse's

Angels of Nature

Edited by Stephen Isaac, Ph.D.

QUEST BOOKS
The Theosophical Publishing House

Wheaton, IL U.S.A./Madras, India

The Theosophical Publishing House
P.O. Box 270
Wheaton, IL 60189–0270

A publication of the Theosophical Publishing House,
a department of the Theosophical Society in America.

*This publication made possible with
the assistance of the Kern Foundation*

Library of Congress Cataloging-in-Publication Data

Newhouse, Flower Arlene Sechler, 1909–1994.
   [Angels of nature]
   Flower A. Newhouse's Angels of nature / edited by Stephen Isaac, Ph.D.
     p. cm.
   "Quest books."
   Includes index.
   ISBN 0-8356-0721-6: $12.00
   1. Newhouse, Flower Arlene Sechler, 1909–1994. 2. Christward Ministry.
   3. Angels—Cult. 4. Mysticism—United States—History—20th century.
   I. Isaac, Stephen, 1925– .
   BP605.C5N379 1995
   253'.3—dc20

94-46683
CIP

9 8 7 6 5 4 3 2 1 * 95 96 97 98 99

Acknowledgments

A book of this nature is the product of a number of individuals who contributed to its research, writing, word processing, and editing. The editor wishes particularly to thank Evelyn Alemanni, Gwen Hulbert, Phyllis Isaac, Hal Lingerman, and Jonathan Wiltshire for their uncounted hours of assistance over several months. Appreciation is also extended to Dr. Mary Clark for excerpts of an unpublished manuscript based on notes taken on trips to New Zealand and Australia with the Rev. Flower A. Newhouse and to Flower's daughter, Athene Bengtson, for selected stories and anecdotes.

Stephen Isaac, Ph.D.
Questhaven Retreat

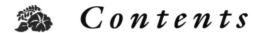

Contents

❧ *Preface*

Angels are found in the sacred books and beliefs of nearly all world religions. The cultures of the past—Egyptian, Greek, Roman, and Persian—and the faiths of today—Muslim, Shinto, Hindu, Kabalist, Maori, and Christian—all accept the reality of Angels and place a special importance on their presence.

The Old and New Testaments of the Bible pay tribute to Angels' existence and service. In our own time, too, the mystical perceptions of divinely inspired persons provide insights into divine reality. Mystics share with us revelations of a world of light and beauty which moves in and about our physical planet. The great naturalist John Muir was gifted in this way. Few have expressed so eloquently our need to reverence God in nature. Muir told us to "Go up to the mountains and breathe the air the Angels breathe." Few have possessed such depth of sight, born of appreciation for the world's beauty. His loving and perceptive eyes saw great rocks as altars and majestic trees as priests which "seem ever to be addressing the surrounding forest."

Among Christian mystics, no one has given a more authoritative and inspired insight into the realm of Angels and their relation to nature and humanity than Flower A. Newhouse. Her clairvoyant sight penetrated beyond physical barriers to reveal an earth peopled not only by Angels, but by nature beings, exquisitely small and dainty, moving in harmony with the soft, diffused music of the heavens. Visiting forests and mountains, she found not lonely and uninhabited places, but realms of great peace and power, populated by tall, graceful beings who hover over trees, lakes, and mountain ranges. Her teachings on the Angel kingdom, which began in the early part of this century, describe glorious inner shrines, temples, and playgrounds from which pure beings broadcast radiations intended to uplift and unfold life on this planet.

We humans are the recipients of gracious gifts that come hourly through the glories and favors of nature. And, we are indirectly influenced and enriched by the ministry of those shining presences called the Angels of nature.

The Angels of nature cause a continuous renaissance in the natural world. They supervise the elements and the seasons. The law of cause and effect ordains the kind of ministry the earth deserves to receive. Thus, these Angels cannot prevent earthquakes or floods, though they can bring rain or calm. When humankind ignorantly or heedlessly commits an error toward the earth, for example, farming without regard to the effects on the soil, the Angels of nature are not permitted to interfere with the inevitable result of soil erosion. Were the Great Ones allowed to prevent natural catastrophes, we humans would not learn the right use and care of the blessings with which nature has endowed us.

Flower A. Newhouse's spiritual example teaches us what is required to develop the intuition and inner perception to sense and appreciate the presence of angelic servers and to recognize and benefit from their instructions. Learning about the great orders of Angels enlarges our inward horizons and deepens our faith. We should welcome every authentic insight into the angelic realm, for humankind will always need the counsel and assistance of those who are pure and beneficent.

Blessings from these holy enlighteners will touch all who love and reverence God more than self and material things. What we receive from Angels in instruction or revelation always increases our understanding of ourselves and our responsiveness to divine wonders.

About Flower A. Newhouse

Flower A. Newhouse—mystic, seer, and metaphysical teacher—was an unforgettable woman gifted with clairvoyance, whose lesson to her pupils was always *herself living the way.* She brought into the world an exceptional synthesis of inner perception, Christian character, and a life consecrated to the rediscovery of esoteric truth. It is from her insights that this book is derived.

Flower's life mission was separating truth from myth to nourish in humankind a more inclusive comprehension of the wondrous range of God-life which invisibly serves and supports life on earth. From childhood she devoted her life to exploring the deeper mysteries and then fearlessly shared her findings through lectures and writings. She worked and taught in this way long before there was any widespread interest in Angels.

One of Flower's early clairvoyant experiences occurred at the age of six, as she rode the Staten Island Ferry to New York. Suddenly, her face brightened. Dancing across the water were dozens of tiny water sprites. In delight, she tugged at the arm of a friend, exclaiming, "Oh, look at the beautiful fairies!" Her companion, blind to such wonders, mistook this for a game of make-believe and gleefully responded with other fanciful inventions. A look of puzzlement came over Flower's face.

As long as Flower could remember, she had seen nature beings and other marvels even more glorious.

The water sprites still skimmed over the waves, but the things her friend described were nowhere to be seen. Then Flower was struck by the perplexing discovery that her friend was making up everything. Painfully, the truth crept to the surface of her mind. She saw a world that others couldn't. Reluctantly, she decided that she would no longer speak of inner realities to those around her. She would close the gate. Like the lovely flowers in a secret garden, her visions would remain her own private sanctuary.

The gate remained closed until her first year in high school. Her class assignments included many compositions, which released the floodgates of her inner seeings. Out flowed insights and experiences that amazed her teachers with their depth and revelation.

Taken by Flower's unaccountable gift, three of her teachers asked if she would be willing to start a series of truth classes, meeting in their homes. It was an opportunity affording an impressive glimpse of what was to come. The years of silence about the inner worlds collapsed, and her work was underway.

What Flower perceived in the world of light inspired and humbled her, giving her the patience and faith to work quietly, knowing that humanity would one day realize the need for a spiritual appreciation of this planet and God's invisible creations which enrich it. She pledged to increase the world's knowledge and awareness of the Angels from whom humankind and nature receive assistance, protection, and encouragement.

Her teachings reveal the vast orders of celestial beings who selflessly serve every element of life, their appearances, responsibilities, and the nature of the assistance they provide to plant, animal, and human life. Through her insights we learn that everywhere we go, the work of Angels surrounds us, for they keep the earth green, productive, and beautiful. The wind, weather, and landscape conform to their movements and directions. Even the transition of the seasons is influenced by Angels in charge of the quarterly changes.

Flower continued to teach and lecture, founding The Christward Ministry. By 1940, she and her husband Lawrence pioneered an isolated valley as a spiritual retreat that would become a permanent home for the ministry. Questhaven Retreat in the hills of Escondido, in southern California, has grown to 640 acres of native coastal chaparral, with nature trails and facilities that attract thousands of visitors each year. Students, teachers, ministers, scholars, and artists come from far places for inner renewal and spiritual instruction.

From this center, Flower carried on her teaching and training ministry. She gave hundreds of talks about the Angels, all available on tape, and authored books, including *Here Are Your Answers, Rediscovering the Angels, Kingdom of the Shining Ones, Insights Into Reality,* and others. This book includes material from these sources, along with excerpts from Flower's lectures, articles, and personal notes filed in Questhaven's archives or provided by other individuals.

On the subject of Angels, Flower was decades ahead of her time, but her outreach as a teacher encompassed more than this fascinating kingdom. She was known first and foremost as a Christian mystic. The bulk of her work centered around Christ and discipleship. She readily recalled her incarnation in His lifetime, and her clairvoyance brought back vivid insights into His ministry. When, for example, Christ spoke of "other sheep I have which are not of this fold," Flower explained, He was referring to the Angels. It was Flower's life mission, first, to rekindle the flames of Christian mysticism and, second, to rediscover the reality of the Angelic Hosts. In their pursuit, it was Flower's custom to journey to many of the earth's holy centers and nature shrines to experience their energies clairvoyantly. These travels particularly were planned to include mountain citadels which were her favorite sources of renewal. She was often accompanied by groups of her followers, making the journey a spiritual pilgrimage whose purpose was to appreciate the earth's holiness and beauty. After a long and eventful life, Flower made her transition in 1994 at the age of 85.

Flower left two legacies to future generations. First, is Questhaven Retreat, a wilderness preserve with miles of enchanting nature trails for spiritual reflection and renewal, the Church of the Holy Quest, Friendship House, and a variety of overnight accommodations for individual guests and retreat groups. Second, is her collected works, including audio and video tapes of her lectures over the years and her numerous books and publications.

Questhaven Retreat is open year-round and conducts an active program of worship services, workshops, and weekend retreats.

Readers who wish more information should contact:

Questhaven Retreat
20560 Questhaven Road
Escondido, CA 92029
(619) 744–1500

About the Illustrations

       The illustrations in this book were painted by Jonathan Wiltshire. Since 1975, Jonathan has served as the principal illustrator for Flower's writings on the Angel world and the inner worlds. Inspired by Flower's clairvoyance, Jonathan relies on intuition to capture images that stream into his awareness. Flower confirmed the inner world authenticity of his art, giving it unique significance.

About the Editor

Dr. Stephen Isaac has been a teacher, counselor, and special consultant in various public schools, universities, and private industries. After earning his B.A. from the University of California at Berkeley, he received an M.A. in clinical psychology and a Ph.D. in experimental psychology from the Claremont Graduate School in Claremont, California.

Dr. Isaac has maintained a life-long interest in Christian mysticism, Questhaven Retreat, and the Reverend Flower A. Newhouse, whom he met when he was ten years old. Ordained a minister in this work in 1952, he serves Questhaven as an instructor, speaker, writer, counselor, and director.

An Angel of the Heights

Chapter 1

 Rediscovering the Angels

A wonderful awakening is beginning to stir the hearts of spiritual seekers everywhere. Like a light shining in dark times, we can sense a growing need to recognize, appreciate, and invite the service of Angels for humanity and our earth. Many of us have already discovered that a reverent inclusion of these selfless servers in our thoughts can lift, purify, and enlighten our daily lives.

People have always known that human beings are not God's only creation. Ancient people, who were natural receptors of eternal truths, accepted superphysical realities as they accepted sunshine and rain, but added to this recognition their own embellishments born of fears, superstitions, and conflicts.

Though their accounts of the reality of Angels may have been inaccurate and fanciful, within old myths and legends we find flashes of truth which have long enriched humanity's interest in the activities of God's celestial emissaries. The ancients understood Angels to exist under the guise of gods and goddesses who dwelt in great idyllic citadels, such as Olympus, Elysium, Valhalla, Nirvana, and Paradise. Though they confounded the angelic nature with an intermingling of human motives, ambitions, and rivalries, the ancients retained in their beliefs a glimmering of the Angels' divine power and spiritual purity.

The sacred books of the world's great religions all contain references to Angels. Among the books of the Old Testament, Genesis, Exodus, Daniel, Psalms, and Zechariah often mention such beings, as do the gospels of Luke and Matthew, along with Acts and Revelation. Richest of all is the Book of Enoch in the Apocrypha, which mentions Angels more often than any of the other ancient scripts. Mohammed, the prophet of Islam, received the Koran from the Archangel Gabriel. The sacred books of India are full of references to angelic beings called devas.

Of the many references to Angels in the New Testament, some give a sense of their luminous aspect. Take for instance, the following passage from the book of Revelation:

> *And I saw another mighty Angel come down*
> *from heaven, clothed with a cloud: and a rainbow was on*
> *his head, and his face was as it were the sun, and his feet*
> *as pillars of fire.*
>
> Rev. 10:1

"Clothed with a cloud" suggests the expansive aura of an Angel, and likening the Angel's face to the sun and feet to pillars of fire is typical of the bright radiance such a being presents to one who is clairvoyant. Colors of the rainbow are also reflected in the countenance of Angels.

As to their number, we have but to turn to the rich descriptions of Angels found in the Book of Enoch in the Apocrypha:

> *And round about were Seraphim, Cherubim, and Ophannin:*
> *And these are they that sleep not,*
> *And guard the throne of His glory.*
> *And I saw angels who could not be counted,*
> *A thousand thousands, and ten thousand times ten thousand,*
> *Encircling the house.*
> *And Michael, and Raphael, and Gabriel, and Phannuel,*
> *And the holy angels who are above the heavens,*
> *Go in and out of that house.*
>
> Book of Enoch, LXXI: 7-8

Greek mythology, while humanizing the gods beyond resemblance to Angels in most instances, nevertheless tells of five races of humans, the first of which—a golden race created by the Titans—rings true as a description of Angels. They lived in ease and tranquility, never having to toil, suffer disease, or grow old. In time, they become benevolent spirits dwelling on earth, who were guardians of humankind, protectors against evil, and sources of abundance—altogether, an idealistic conception of Guardian Angels.

Given the ample evidence of Angels in holy books and historical records, what more proof of their existence is needed? Two problems seem to prevent many people from appreciating the reality of Angels. First, in the minds of many people, Angels are understood to be an historical phenomenon that has no place in contemporary times. Yes, we read Bible stories in which they play a role, but such events took place long ago and far away—nothing to do with our own times. From this point of view, God called upon angelic beings for a limited period of service, including taking part in the events of the Bible; then their intervention in the affairs of the world was concluded. Second, the Bible and other existing records contain very little to describe the appearance or the nature of Angels or the purpose they serve. Whatever descriptions have survived are fragmentary and awe-inspiring. If Angels exist at all, some people are forced to conclude that they must be extraordinary beings, altogether as mysterious and fascinating as the discovery of an advanced civilization on a distant planet.

Against this background, it is clear that if we are to believe in Angels, we will want to know more about their kind of existence, what they look like, what they do and, most particularly, how their lives relate to ours. Christian mystic and clairvoyant Flower A. Newhouse spent her lifetime observing and communicating with these wondrous presences. In her many lectures and books about Angels, we learn that the angelic world is a vast kingdom—an entire line of evolution complementing humanity.

Flower taught that Angels are arranged in both hierarchical orders and branches of service. The hierarchical orders based on their degree of unfoldment are already familiar to us: Angels, Archangels, Principalities, Powers, Virtues, Dominions, Thrones, Cherubim, and Seraphim. Note that the orders making up the angelic kingdom are more advanced than their human counterparts, since the lowest-ranking Angel is equivalent to a person attaining sainthood in human spiritual evolution. As a consequence, the human mind cannot fathom beings much beyond Archangel rank. The number of Angels approaches infinity, as they are the principal means of coordinating the universe, in service to their Creator.

Four branches or waves of this kingdom are attuned primarily to physical existence and to the service of life active on the planet. The first of these is the nature wave. It is this branch that is the principal focus of this book, and it will be described in some detail in the chapters that follow. The second is called the life motivation wave, which is concerned with the destiny of both humans and animals. The third wave is associated with the release of divine wisdom under the direction of the Holy Spirit. The fourth, known as the wave of love, is ruled by the Lord Christ.

What Angels Look Like

Angels are composed of radiant light energies that cause them to be instantly recognizable as beings from another world. What is most memorable is their large and luminous eyes which send forth beams of purest love. A single glance from any Angel is enough to bring us to our knees, if it is our fortune to behold one. On the other hand, Angels do not seek or accept the worship of humans. This is reserved for God alone, and Angels quietly, unobtrusively turn aside from any well-intentioned human overtures.

Angels are alive in a way that is utterly refreshing to observe. They exhibit no idleness, no wasted effort, no casualness. At the same time, there is no hurry or excitement in their movements—just a smooth flow of activity, unhesitating

A Guardian of Sedona

and, to our eyes, magical. They exude a refinement and purity that, even if sensed intuitively, transforms the recipient. They are in truth the ideal beings celebrated in myths and legends, who come from a perfect kingdom and who deserve our unstinting admiration and recognition. They are as real as the air we breathe, though just as invisible.

Flower has described the happiness of Angels. They smile, but not in the amused or giddy manner typical of humans. Their smile comes from their very souls, and with the smile shines forth a burst of color, a combination of burnished gold and peach, if you can imagine such a blending. Their smile radiates from their whole being and, if you are touched by it, you will know the kind of happiness that Angels know. Angels experience such happiness when they witness a human with whom they have worked finally rise above an entrenched bad habit.

Jonathan Wiltshire, the artist who created the illustrations for this book, recalls a conversation he had with Flower about the appearance of nature devas and Angels. In contrast to artistic tradition, he had drawn devas so that the top of the head, beginning just above the eyes, was shaped like an upturned crescent. Flower confirmed the impression, saying it resembled the devic presences she had seen in the Sedona region of Arizona—very fiery, emanating powerful energies.

He also recalls Flower's comments regarding Angels' relationship with people. First of all, they are largely unaware of humans unless the person enters their dominion with a sense of reverence and humility. When this is true, the person's aura is expanded, luminous, and afire with color. The Angels or devas in the vicinity notice such an individual, much like one of us hiking on a mountain trail would notice a precious ruby or diamond sparkling in the sunlight amidst the background of undistinguished stones. So it is that if we enter nature reverently, Angels will recognize that we are worthy of their appreciation.

Once Flower was asked, "What do you consider the greatest benefit in seeing an Angel?" She answered, "To see one glorified being is to remember always the meaning of beauty, the power of love, and the blessedness of sincerity. The sight of one who reflects the light more completely and consciously than ourselves is our challenge to greater effort." As is so often true of mystics, Flower was brief in her comments, seldom going into detail and leaving much for the pupil to contemplate. As a teacher, she also answered queries in a way that pointed to one's next step of growth.

Of the many misrepresentations humankind has imposed on Angels, perhaps the most distorted are paintings presenting them as little children or "cherubic" babies. Nothing could be further from the truth. Angels are, by contrast, tall and awesome in their majesty and power, in some instances standing thirty feet in height. Another misconception commonly appearing in paintings of Angels is the inclusion of wings. This feature undoubtedly has come about partly because of our tendency to project upon Angels the need to fly, as if wings therefore would be necessary. The truth is, Angels move by willing it. A more compelling reason exists for this confusion. Angels have vivid, expansive, and constantly moving auras of light which resemble wings. Artists, experiencing glimpses of these otherwise invisible beings, understandably have mistaken the outlines of their auras for the wings we so often see portrayed in paintings.

The faces of most angelic beings are rather elongated. Their eyes can be likened to deep pools, with occasional flashes of lightning. Angels absorb electricity from the etheric regions of the earth's atmosphere; this sustains them in the same way as oxygen sustains us. The feeling one has while observing these pure beings, according to Flower, is a yearning for the tremendous vitality with which they are endowed. Angels, she has taught, are always joyous, confident, and sympathetic.

How Angels' Lives Compare to Ours

The angelic line of evolution distinguishes itself from the human line in a number of ways. Angels usually are invisible, manifesting themselves only to those who have the gift of inner perception. The exceptions are the relatively rare occasions when they take on human form to intervene to save a life or otherwise to make a difference in the well-being of worthy individuals. Angels serve God with complete obedience to divine will. The free will which humans cherish and which allows an individual to choose a course of action or inaction that may not always be in conformity with God's will, slows human progress in the early to middle stages of evolution, but greatly accelerates it once that will is surrendered to God—an attribute of every great soul.

Evolution in the angelic kingdom, while slow in contrast to that of humans, is steadfast and harmonious, rendering its inhabitants joyous, purposeful, and marvelously beneficial. Theirs is also an older evolution than our own. Angels do not have to endure a childhood as humans do, for once they achieve angelhood, such beings come into a state of existence that is permanently mature and ever unfolding. They no longer face cycles of death and rebirth. They exist in a state of eternal youthfulness, strength, and untiring service.

Angels are especially important to our evolution because they understand our destiny and our potentialities in ways that we do not. They see our life plan, and it is their mission to help this plan come into fruition. Thus, they are constantly intersecting our lives with promptings and interventions that open up possibilities that, if left unattended, we would miss. It is important that we lift our thoughts to them, because they unceasingly, devoutly, joyously, and selflessly work on behalf of all life on earth, ourselves included.

For example, from about the time she was ten years old, Flower's Guardian Angel sent her frequent promptings to enhance her upbringing—to join the Girl Scouts, attend a variety of church services and cultural events, even spend her meager resources ordering a bowl of soup in the finest restaurants, thus acquiring a foundation in the social graces.

The most valuable lesson we can learn from Angels is that of selfless service. Altruism is the most salient feature of life in their kingdom and, at the same time, the most absent feature of life among humans. Angels are unreservedly given to their adoration of God. There has never been a time that they have not striven to know God's will and to do it exactly. They have direct and uninterrupted access to truth and are open at all times to the fertile, glorious, and ever-abundant energies of divine intelligence.

What Angels Do

Flower's keenest impression of Angels is of their tenderness, compassion, and blinding purity. These qualities are not directed at humans any more than to animals or trees. The growing things of earth receive the same measure of care from these wondrous beings as do the most innocent or needy individuals. Angels simply give their all to everything in God's creation, holding nothing back.

Angels serve enthusiastically and selflessly. They are not afflicted with a personality self which stubbornly, pridefully, and foolishly goes its own way. They do not suffer from egos that are ambitious or fearful or petty. They exist solely for the glory of God and for divine righteousness.

We are unceasingly in the presence of Angels, wherever we are, because their mission is the well-being of life on earth. They far outnumber us—a remarkable fact in itself to dwell upon—and are instantly aware of our needs and our receptivity. Whenever we are facing tests or adverse circumstances, angelic assistance is immediately present, whether we are conscious of their ministrations or not. During the holy days observed by the world's religions, special dispensations are administered by these glorious beings that revitalize the commitment of worshipers. Wherever there are leaders making important decisions, Angels converge to influence the outcome. And as disappointing as the results of many of these human deliberations seem to be, imagine how much worse things might be had none of their number been involved.

Most of all, Angels are present in our ordinary, everyday lives, waiting and watching for signs of our readiness to understand and to learn, to achieve insight and to resolve to change that which needs changing. If there are emergencies or trials, if we are in any danger, Angels are immediately at our side. In fact, were we to know the countless ministrations offered by these servers from the inner worlds, we would be aghast, so frequent and so numerous are their interventions. In return for the gift of their watchfulness, there is no finer gift for us to return to them than our gratitude.

With few exceptions, Angels rely on our intuitions to instruct us. Human thought, especially its more creative expressions, often is the work of the Guardian Angel or Angels that serve the Holy Spirit. They create ethereal energy fields known as thought forms; these enter the mental region of the human aura, prompting the consciousness of receptive individuals to become aware of their presence. The result is a thought that comes to us "out of the blue" — a reliable sign that, not our own cleverness, but the inspiration of a higher intelligence was its source. Even when such ideas come to us from the realms of Angels, we do not always receive them undiminished, and some portion of the message may get lost in translation.

It might seem strange that with all their concern for our protection from harm or misadventure, things nevertheless go wrong in our lives. If Angels are so capable and omnipresent, why isn't life on earth smoother and safer? The truth is, Angels cannot interfere with our free will. They can call things to our attention, warn us, or inspire us, but they are not allowed to overrule our unwise choices or ill-advised actions. Furthermore, if a karmic debt falls due because of mistakes in the past, the most that Angels can do is to comfort us and help us meet the obligation constructively.

The Nature Wave

Most of what has been shared to this point concerns the three waves of Angels who work directly with humanity and its unfoldment. The remaining wave of the Angel kingdom is the nature wave, and its distinguishing feature is its preoccupation with the four elements: earth, air, water, and fire. From the nature wave as well originate the younger forms of nature beings, who eventually evolve through the deva line into Angels serving in any one of the four principal waves. Nature, then, is the seedbed out of which the Creator brings forth new generations of angelic servers.

The youngest of these forms of nature beings are called elementals—tiny entities who permeate the planet and who literally breathe life and health into all that makes up the four natural realms. Each realm—earth, air, water, and fire—is home to a sequence of beings that ascend toward devahood, the final stage of evolution in becoming an Angel.

For the most part, nature beings and Angels of this wave focus on their native domain, and their contact with humans is incidental. Certainly, when we are attentive and respectful of these servers, they recognize this quality and appreciate us, but otherwise humankind is in the distant background. An exception to this rule often occurs when we abuse nature or treat it carelessly, a behavior that can result in natural disasters or personal misfortune, in which the Angels of nature must become involved. In the main, however, nature is a world unto itself, toward which we now turn our attention.

The Forest's Inner Inhabitants

Chapter 2

 Nature's Open Door

Of the four great waves of angelic beings serving life on earth, the wave of nature is the most diverse in its inhabitants and its activities. Because so many of us lack an intimate relationship with this sphere, it is vitally important to bridge the gap that separates the world of nature from the world of human affairs. An appreciation of the Angels of nature can help us accomplish this.

Too many humans accept nature casually rather than with an expectation of its benefits. They enjoy nature's scenery and her recreational opportunities but do not realize her capacities for enlightenment and transformation. They miss nature's great gift to awakened souls—a palette with which to paint masterpieces of experience and revelation. To attain the level of awareness at which such high art is possible, one begins by learning to sense beyond the surface of nature's many realms, reaching instead into the heartbeat of each moment.

A secret in this quest for illumination is the realization that when one experiences nature through the eyes of inner perception, there is nothing commonplace in this kingdom. The poet and mystic William Blake captured this truth when he wrote of our ability "to see a world in a grain of sand/and a heaven in a wild flower."

Such an approach to nature requires reverence. In contrast to a casual or indifferent attitude, the sensitive individual looks upon nature as a sacred creation of God that deserves to be valued and revered. Once God's creation is appreciated, nature becomes our teacher, indeed, our priestess. This has been the experience of a long line of mystic-naturalists, from Henry David Thoreau and John Muir to Edwin Way Teale, John Burroughs, Sam Campbell, Hal Borland, and others. These pioneers of nature mysticism should be read and reread, for they are pathfinders to humanity's nascent yet unfolding wisdom about nature. Flower reminds us that to benefit from the wilderness experience, we should read one of these prophets every year. She suggests that we mark those passages that open our eyes to nature's truths and review them before setting out on holidays or vacations into nature's dominions.

An excellent opportunity to begin our discovery of God in nature comes during our vacations. These periods of relaxation from external duties and routines give us the occasion to

Hikers Enter Nature's
Open Door

journey into places that hold the promise of inner renewal and revelation. Ideally, our vacation should be an opportunity to behold God's handwriting in the majesty of mountains, the solemnity of forests, the tranquility of lakes, the joy of running brooks, and the splendor of flower-strewn meadows. Vacations allow us to venture into wilderness regions of God's great outdoors, with the wish that the scales be removed from our eyes, and our ears be tuned to hear in the sounds of nature the subtle reverberations of the music of the spheres. With our inner senses opened, the signs and symbols of nature reveal the language of God in all its delightful rhythms—in the songs of the wind through the trees and in the calls of the birds.

As our motives become more refined and worshipful, intimations of truths and insights into creation transform who we are. We may even be touched by a timeless moment, transporting us into another dimension in which we become one with the Creator. Individuals favored with such a moment of revelation report not only the suspension of time, but the emergence of an iridescent inner beauty in otherwise common objects such as trees and flowers.

Whatever our experience, what counts is the transformation of our motives and our expectations as we enter nature. Our ignorance and our superficiality—the two most familiar enemies of enlightenment—can be swept away by an experience of nature's true glory. Having reached this threshold, we become pupils of our inner senses and learn to look and listen for all that nature teaches.

One of the most important benefits of nature is its healing power. Not simply our bodies, but our troubled emotions and burdened minds respond to nature's restorative energies. If we are depleted and need recharging, we are best served by visiting mountains. Should we be tense and overcharged with nervous energy, the sea should be our destination. As long as we are respectful of her domain, nature is accepting and supportive. We needn't worry about making the right impression or about not measuring up to expectations. We step into nature's habitat easily. Whatever our need may be for returning to wholeness, we will find ourselves with a sympathetic caretaker. Then, if we reach that state of highest reverence and unity with this glorious kingdom, we reach a point that takes us outside of ourselves. What happens next is healing of the finest order. Emptied of self-preoccupations, we are marvelously cleansed and freed of indifference, pettiness, meanness, and aggression. As a result, we are truly humbled, and in that humility is born a bond with nature linking our voice with the myriads of other voices praising God and the wonders of creation.

Nature is an ideal medium for healing because of its purity and reservoirs of power. While the work of the Angels of nature is not directly the healing of humans, they are nevertheless drawn to individuals who are open and receptive to regeneration. One order of the Angels is specifically charged with healing; these are the beings who respond to the prayers or unspoken needs of individuals. The role of the Angels of nature is to reside in natural settings that emanate rejuvenating energies that attract those of us who seek an uplift or surge of well-being.

The Energies of Nature's Kingdom

The diverse energies in nature's kingdom gives each mountain range, each tree, each geographic or ecological region its own distinct emanation. Discerning the radiances that are the signature qualities of particular settings is a rewarding adventure. Mountains, for example, offer a variety of energies. A particular mountain may dispense the light of God into the atmosphere, making it an attractive place for meditation on enlightenment. Another mountain may be a repository of power, which is able to recharge every atom of one's being. A third may be an initiatory mountain whose effect is to facilitate conquering the ego. Wherever you find yourself, wherever nature is on display, quiet yourself and ask to be shown the keynote of this particular spot. Do not be impatient for an answer; when you are at peace with yourself and humbly receptive, impressions will come.

Out of this immense kingdom that governs nature—its countless beings and presences—emerges a mighty flow of creative energy, inexhaustible and irresistible, the etheric fuel nourishing all life. When we enter nature's sanctuaries, our own auras are magnetically recharged in these reservoirs of energy. Thus just as nature is the source of warmth, sustenance, and shelter for our physical bodies, it also nourishes our emotions, minds, and souls.

Like mountains, trees have unique and important energies. Next to the animals and human beings, trees may be the most important form of life on the planet. The more we love trees, the closer we come to the recognition of the tree devas who watch over them. Tree devas are a fascinating company of servers who are at a stage of unfoldment in the nature kingdom equivalent to most humans. We gain access to their acquaintance through a genuine love of the trees they care for. Every time we plant a tree, we widen the circle of their service and earn their benedictions.

Flower exemplified the preciousness of trees on a memorable occasion at Questhaven Retreat some years ago. She had outgrown her residence, or so it seemed to her Board of Directors, and was offered a new home in a location of her choice with up-to-date features. She thought it over for a few days, then turned down the offer. She said she appreciated the opportunity, but she couldn't bear to leave the trees she had planted and loved.

The most advanced of trees are the evergreens, which likewise attract the most advanced devas. Groves of redwoods and sequoias are particularly mantled with devas that are transcendent to behold. To stand in the presence of such mighty giants is to be in a holy cathedral of overpowering beauty. Nothing fashioned by human hands quite compares to the sanctity of great trees.

Wherever we go in nature, communion is continuously taking place. If we are observant, we will sense how alert and attentive are trees themselves, especially ones which are the home of devas. These beings respond to humans who approach a forest with reverence, appreciation, and holy expectancy. How sad it is that so many people are ignorant and insensitive to this simple fact: all living things are linked, and trees are particularly blessed and interconnected with other life because of their affinity for devas. To prove this to ourselves, we need only think of the experience of watering a tree on a parched summer day. The aura of the tree fairly shimmers in delight and thanksgiving.

There is also much to be said for visiting new places, new mountains or forests, even new countries. The freshness of such experiences is stimulating. We enjoy the thrill of discovery

when we enter new regions, particularly if the terrain is distinctive or its trees or high places have unique appeal. In planning trips of this kind, it is important to research what lies ahead and to select the particular locations that have promise, recognizing at the same time that some of our finest experiences come quite by surprise. It is also worthwhile if we can locate writings by naturalists familiar with the regions we wish to visit to benefit from their experience.

If we stop to think about it, what is so distinctive about nature is its peace and acceptance. The biblical passage, "the peace of God that passeth all understanding" seems most apt in an alpine meadow, on a mountain summit, in the cathedral setting of a great forest, or in another such sanctuary in God's creation. Acceptance is another of nature's hallmarks. Young or old, rich or poor, good looking or plain, nature's arms are open to us, regardless of our talents or handicaps. We are neither favored with preferential treatment nor subject to neglect or rejection. Moreover, the great theme of nature is the cycle of rebirth and renewal. We see it in the rising and setting of the sun and the passing of the seasons, and we feel it in our own lives as we strive toward the horizon of our personal future.

Harvesting Nature's Bounty

A Flower Fairy

So it is that more than physical sight is required to begin to harvest the bounty that awaits us in nature. One has to be attuned through reverence and expectantly alert to catch sight of her limitless treasures. Nor is our entry into such deep seeing a threshold we cross once and for all. More often it comes in increments, like ascending a staircase. What we receive is fundamentally a function of our own growth—the gradual expansion of our awareness and the refinement of our motives. In order to receive more, we must give more in the form of our own unfoldment. Then, each time we go into a place that is pure and powerfully charged, it may be our good fortune to experience more than before.

In the divine reckoning of the Creator, we are judged not according to our worldly attainments of fame or fortune, rank or degrees; we are judged solely on the basis of the inner growth we have achieved according to the truth we have touched. Individuals who advance more rapidly are those who have given themselves more completely to what has been learned—who discover each unique facet of revealed truth with nature and then apply it swiftly and wholeheartedly to their lives. To such individuals nature will dispense her great secrets.

Flower has described what happens to the aura when we enter a magnificent natural setting. Normally constricted to a width of only a few inches, in response to the beauty of a mountain vastness or other awe inspiring scenery, the aura doubles or triples its width and is infused with a radiance of colors that sparkle iridescently. As the perceiver ventures deeper into a nature wonderland, the aura begins to absorb the hues that characterize the locale. The purity and vibrance that come with these hues bring a sense of peace and revitalization that originates with the activity of the Angels and nature beings inhabiting this region. For us, this comes as a fortuitous gift, for these glorious presences are so absorbed in their service to nature, they normally do not notice humans entering their domain. To hear Flower describe it, having one's aura cleansed and recharged with angelic energies, the colors of which are often beyond the range of our visible spectrum, is much like taking a magical shower.

Flower also reports that we collect in our auras archetypal images that reflect the particular character of nature beings in certain locations. For example, a couple close to Flower visited the remote White Mountain range of central California, home of the bristlecone pine, the world's oldest trees. The setting is above ten thousand feet, windblown and austere, but pristine and unspoiled. On their return, Flower was fascinated to see crystalline symbols in their auras that mirrored these most unusual nature beings. The effect of these symbols was mentally invigorating.

A most appropriate time to enter nature for instruction is on one's birthday. At such a time we are apt to be more receptive, more attuned, and more appreciative. If we are fortunate, on such an occasion nature will endow us with a glimpse of what lies ahead, what cycle we will be entering, and what needs transcending in our lives. It is a day to be open to receive intuitive promptings and insights.

Nature has no favorites. Whenever we are most humble, we will learn the most. For us to receive, our auras must be open like tendrils or like a sunburst. We are then available to glorious impressions all about us. The more ways we have of finding God, the more we absorb and the less we are pre-occupied with thoughts of ourselves which otherwise crowd out the gifts of inner sensitivity.

To be a true nature mystic whose receptivity is steadfast, our struggle with self-centeredness must be a never-ending discipline. Being in tune with the eyes of our soul arouses ever-increasing degrees of self-giving.

Nature's messages are everywhere visible to us, if only we will open our hearts to her reality. Each of us, in looking back over our lives, should write down in our journals those golden moments we have received in her presence. We owe that much to posterity so that those who come after us will have footprints to follow into nature's realms.

There is so much to learn in nature's kingdom. If patience is our lesson, we could find no better teacher, for nature's patience in watching the slow pace of the passing seasons is example enough. If our lesson is tolerance, her acceptance of the diversity of life forms is unexcelled. If our lesson is caring, she surpasses our human capacities by magnitudes beyond counting. And so it goes. If we are wise, we will take our troubles, whatever they are, into some nature sanctuary, to find answers there that come in no other way. Better still, troubled or not, let us establish with nature a kinship that we can experience frequently and profoundly as a permanent part of our life.

If we reverence nature, she will be at our side like the mother she is. Then, the rising sun, rain, moonlight, the change of seasons, a great and friendly tree, the pattern of snowflakes, the wildness and scent of winds, the loveliness of the most miniature flower will cheer us immensely and fill us with a sublime awareness of our Creator who, to our amazement and for the sake of divine delight, fashions such wonders even in places human eyes never reach.

A Frakin Breathes Life into the Morning Glory

Chapter 3

 The Realm of Earth

In this chapter we begin looking through the eyes of Flower at the four realms of the nature kingdom—earth, air, water, and fire. We will discover that each realm contains its own hierarchy of enchanting beings, from tiny elementals performing the most fundamental activities, to exalted Angels watching over vast territories within their sphere of responsibility. We will also learn that just as humans are under the care of Watcher or Guardian Angels, all of nature's growing things and even its minerals are tirelessly attended by a fascinating company of invisible servers.

The entire range of nature beings, Flower taught, possess no free will of the type humans know. God's will alone—the will of the good—is known and heeded. For that reason, throughout the entire Angel kingdom, from the loftiest Angel to the youngest elemental, flows a constant stream of instantaneous obedience to the will of the Highest. For the citizenry of the angelic realm, life and evolution are a slow but certain path.

Under the care of the Angels of the earth realm is everything that grows. From the most humble grasses and delicate mosses to the most exalted redwoods and sequoias, every growing thing is nourished and unfolded by the tender, loving labors of a glorious company of beings. In addition, Angels of this realm also have charge of the less commanding to the eye, but equally important minerals, common and precious, that form the body of our planet.

The Elementals

The first order under the charge of earth Angels is a group of tiny beings known as *elementals*. The inhabitants of each of the four realms evolve from this youngest form of angelic life. In the earth realm, elementals abound as the spirit essence of plants and minerals. Initially, they are minute beings, no larger than a thumbnail. In time, however, they grow to a foot in height. At this stage, they are sentient creatures but have yet to develop intelligence. They nevertheless can feel, sense, and respond instinctively to the directives and promptings of the more advanced beings supervising their activities.

The earth we walk is home to countless elementals. They serve the God force ruling all of nature obediently and without opposition. They cannot comprehend why we humans do not do likewise. Elementals never know weariness, and laziness is absolutely foreign to their experience. Their own advancement in angelic evolution takes place as their enthusiasm ripens and expands, thus increasing their size. The time comes when something akin to intelligence begins to function. At this point they are at the threshold of the stages of devahood.

More stories are told about earth elementals than about the angelic inhabitants of the other natural realms. Elementals appear in fairy tales and have given rise to a wealth of folklore. Irish mythology in particular is rich in tales of the little people, and more recently J.R.R. Tolkien's stories about Bilbo, the Hobbit, and Middle Earth continue this tradition. For their part, elementals see into the motivation of humans, and they often do not like what they see. They are particularly distraught when they encounter a reservoir of destructive human thought or a pile of human-made refuse. Elementals will work to rid the earth of these aberrations, but so consequential is the fallout from misguided human emotions and motives that hurricanes, earthquakes, and all manner of so-called natural disasters often result.

Earth elementals, in particular, are normally charming and precious to behold. The exceptions occur, in Flower's experience, when they have cause to worry about someone's selfishness or the suffering of an animal. Then every part of the affected elemental looks worried and wrinkled. This expression is short-lived, however, as the Angels in charge of these delightful beings remind them to release these feelings at once, as they serve no constructive purpose. They are then encouraged to generate some impetus or impulse for the good that might offset the source of selfishness or suffering.

Flower has noted many earth elementals as she walked out-of-doors. She reports that they are as common as the grasses and flowers. She describes them as a teeming population of lively beings, who take no particular notice of humans as they tirelessly go about their endeavors. These delightfully busy creatures create a sea of luminescent activity across the landscape. Their appearance varies with the locale, but they have in common a light-filled essence that is reminiscent of butterflies fluttering among a field of flowers. Their exquisite little faces radiate a joyous quality. Their hands and feet are also visible, while the rest of what would constitute their bodies often dissolves in soft glowing clusters of light.

The one quality earth elementals expect of humans is unselfishness. Selfishness is beyond their comprehension, and they are strongly repelled by it. One of the most important traits for humans to cultivate in order to harmonize with elementals is generosity. When people are open-hearted and naturally good, Flower has seen tiny elementals actually enter their homes, which is quite a compliment to the human's character.

Elementals contribute to the atmosphere and ambience of the places we live. When we leave our homes and travel to a distant region where elementals are of a different constitution, we often experience a form of homesickness. For instance, when Flower was traveling in the Pacific northwest some years ago, she felt a particular longing for southern California and its habitat. Since she was surrounded by exquisite scenery at the time, this feeling puzzled her, and she was prompted to ask her Guardian Angel what was behind her reaction. The Guardian answered that she missed the energy of the elementals native to the southwest and to Mexico who work with more ardor and enthusiasm. The elementals of the northwestern and eastern United States, she was told, are more passive.

A vast company of elementals also serves throughout the mineral kingdom. What is noteworthy about these industrious beings is the brightness of the area around their hearts, which signifies the wealth of feeling they invest in their selfless labors. Mineral elementals are childlike in body, although their faces are not always youthful. Their work is to nourish and refine the qualities that make each mineral distinctive. They tend to specialize, concentrating on particular minerals such as copper, iron, gold, or silver. Of special interest are those beings associated with precious gemstones which are the culmination of a mineral's perfection, equivalent to redwoods and sequoias in the plant world. However, these devoted servers give the same level of care to all minerals, regardless of their value by worldly standards.

Elementals make their final appearance in the form of frakins, more commonly called fairies. Varying in height from eight to twelve inches, frakins are beautiful creatures possessing a childlike appearance that reflects either their feminine or masculine qualities. Frakins, like all the beings who wear etheric bodies, experience birth and death. Unlike humans, they are not born of mothers. They are fashioned by higher intelligences who create them from elemental essence. They exist in the etheric plane of earth for approximately a century and share responsibility for the flowering plants, grasses, and other smaller forms of vegetable life.

The work of frakins is energizing etherically the simplest cells of life through regular rhythmic breathing, a practice which recharges the earth's surface to a depth of three feet. Etheric breathing, rather than use of the hands, is the customary means by which frakins and other elementals impress, quicken, and energize the plant life in their care.

Flower spent many happy moments observing the work of these delightful creatures. On one occasion, she tells us, "as I walked from my chapel study to our home, I paused at the sight of nearly a hundred elemental creatures flying slowly from flower to flower. Before me was a cover of blue-eyed grass mixed with owl's clover, Indian paint brush, monkey flower and blossoming chemise. There was a delicate lyrical hum over the heads of the blue-eyed grass. I stood enraptured by the loveliness of these busy visitors."

Elves and Gnomes

Ranked above the frakins are the elves. Elves are somewhat larger than frakins, ranging from fifteen to twenty-four inches in height. They are also more vigorous and more clearly defined in form. As with all small angelic creatures, their size increases and decreases as a function of the contraction and expansion of their breathing, a process that is slower and deeper in the world of nature angels than in that of humans. Elves are entrusted with the care of larger plants and shrubs, those which attain a height of twelve feet or more. As elves travel from one growing form in their domain to another, each plant receives a surcharging of the energies circulating through its etheric body; its life is thus maintained and strengthened.

Gnomes are more evolved than elves, and they are larger still. In children's legends and folklore, beings of this general group are occasionally called brownies. Unlike the fanciful image that many people have, such as gnomes wearing quaint human clothing, gnomes prefer to be attired in what appear to be leaves and flowers. They are very responsive to thoughtful direction and are more advanced than the most intelligent domesticated animals. They typically live for as long as three centuries. Among themselves, gnomes have names and experience ecstasies, fears, and disappointments comparable to those of humans.

Gnomes dwell in the etheric world in proximity to the rocks above and below the earth's crust. Their ringing cry of activity is, "Awake! Awake! All sleeping forms be aroused to life!"

To win acceptance and recognition from the angels of nature, we must approach them with genuine interest in their particular fields of service. When an individual evidences a love for the soil and its growing life, its sculptured rocks, majestic mountains, and green forests, such a person comes under the watchful care of nature's angelic guardians. Should one of the gnomes take an interest in a human being, the gnome might disclose one of the particular treasures under his or her care. The treasure might be a simple keepsake or a rich mineral deposit of considerable worth.

Flower has often had experiences while walking in the wilderness, of finding symbolic "treasures"—a beautifully formed piece of wood, a stone, or a piece of bark. Often her attention was drawn to these objects by a gnome or other nature being. Each find would have a special significance. For instance, a piece of wood with a knothole might be a symbol of the third eye of clairvoyance or of seeing an emotional situation clearly, depending on one's consciousness at the time. One time, she brought home a rather large piece of wood, which so clearly resembled a unicorn's head that everyone who saw it assumed that it had been carved by a human artist.

On the other hand, whenever humans poison the etheric energies of nature through pollution or selfish habits, serious karmic consequences result. If out of greed, for example, what was formerly a cherished natural shrine becomes a wasteland, there will be serious repercussions. Those who deal violently with nature are often killed violently by nature. But those who have the wisdom and thankfulness of spirit to enter nature with reverence find a heartwarming return of respect and loyalty.

Whenever Flower has been in nature, she has frequently observed elves and gnomes. One gnome to whom she gave the name "Poppy" was particularly fond of a resident of Questhaven who helped maintain the grounds. The little fellow would follow the groundskeeper around, observing his work and lending a hand in a fun-loving, delightful way. Poppy would sit on a rock and watch sometimes for hours while the gardener worked on a project. Other times he would be playfully distracted by other nature beings, or even by an animal or pet who happened by. Whenever the caretaker was on the retreat grounds, Poppy would not be far away—a most unusual attachment.

Flower also had a Keeshond dog named Liebeling that seemed especially attractive to gnomes. She often observed her dog playing with these nature spirits. One afternoon, when

Flower was reading in her living room, a gnome entered the house. At first Flower didn't see anything, but she heard a voice calling, "Grufla?" The being called out several times and then wandered into the living room. It looked at Flower and then seemed to ask her, "Bobildink?"—a charming introduction to the mysterious language of gnomes. Like the incident with Poppy, the rarity was for a gnome to interact with a human, since they find very few of us engaging. Flower was impressed and amused by this curious encounter.

Tree Devas

Above the gnomes in angelic evolution are the tree devas, a group of advanced nature beings who stand near the threshold of angelhood. Tree devas are often mistaken for Angels by those fortunate enough to glimpse them because of their striking appearance and their vibrant energy and radiance. Devas deserve credit for much of the creation and maintenance of beauty and harmony in nature. They are not only industrious but gifted with intelligence and sensitivity.

Tree devas care for the well-being of trees wherever they are found. Flower once observed that a place without trees appears empty and desolate when viewed clairvoyantly. This emptiness is due in large part to a lack of deva energy. "If only people everywhere would perceive that trees not only give outer beauty to the land," she explained on one occasion, "but their

The Forest Healer

very forms are enveloped by bright intelligences who radiate superphysical energies through the growing trees."

Tree devas are resplendent presences, often as tall as the trees they watch over. While their appearance is not beautiful by classical human standards—their features are too elongated and narrow, and their faces too triangular—they have the equivalent of beauty in their boundless etheric energy.

They appear to humans as light green creatures, with flashing eyes that bombard one with their vitality and penetration. Flower spent several hours at various times watching devas move from tree to tree, giving fully of their charging presence. Persons who love nature often attract their attention and even their baptism of renewal. Where they know they are welcome, tree devas bring an added blessing to the gardens and trees surrounding homes.

Most tree devas are not drawn to the atmosphere of cities, preferring rural and wilderness regions. Nevertheless, some devas do attend to the needs of trees in cities and have adapted themselves to the climate of noise and busyness that typifies the city environment. They work for the benefit of the city's people. Flower recalls one city in particular, near the foot of a mountain range, which contains a magnificent deodar cedar in its central park. A great deva dwells in this tree and is present throughout the day and night, sending forth a most unusual blessing to this city and its inhabitants.

Devas alter their activities in response to the seasons. During the summer months when an influx of people flood into parks and forests, devas withdraw from the more crowded areas and move up the mountain slopes. When summer ends, they make their way back into the lower areas to continue their nurturing work. Fall and winter are the more inward turning seasons, while spring and summer are the most outward turning times, and devas reflect this cycle.

Their own time for renewal is at night when they gather in large numbers in certain mountain regions known as deva playgrounds. The terrain tends to be open, with steep descents, allowing the devas to swoop and soar among the trees, an activity that not only recharges their spirits but fills them with joy and thanksgiving. Flower has seen hundreds of tree devas drawn from an extended territory gather in the late afternoon in such a playground to begin this nightly ritual of recharging.

During her travels, Flower came to appreciate the variation in nature presences who inhabit different regions of the planet. This became especially apparent in her visits to Australia and New Zealand. Tree devas in Australia were taller and more slender than those she was used to observing in the vicinity of Questhaven. Furthermore, she observed that these tree devas were friendly and lovable, as well as intensely curious about Flower and her companions, who were recognized to be visitors from another continent. The Australian devas had auras that gave off a yellow radiance mingled with silver and opalescent hues, some of which were beyond our spectrum. Those of Questhaven possessed a shimmering moonlight green radiance that grew lighter with advancement.

On the west coast of New Zealand's South Island, she noted further differences. Here the forests are dense, and the devas, instead of spacing themselves well apart as Flower was accustomed to, were gathered in clusters. The joy in their faces revealed that they enjoyed this configuration. Like those of Australia, the devas of New Zealand had auras that were predominantly opalescent, growing brighter with their degree of unfoldment.

In their own natural habitat, devas are utterly at home and immerse themselves constantly in the joy of service. They serve obediently under the supervision of Angels who often have large numbers of tree devas under their charge. To humans, even gifted seers like Flower, the appearance and activity of such beings is an awesome spectacle. For instance, when visiting the redwoods, Flower once had the following experience: "I was meditating with my eyes open when I saw a great being appear over a cluster of young redwood trees. Larger than any of the devas in the region, this Angel seemed more like those who attend the ministry of Christ. He was immensely large, his skin was a rosy white, and he had black hair that clung in ringlets about his head. The aura he emanated must have extended for a hundred feet in every direction. This emanation he created was iridescent, and it shone brightly. Seldom have I seen a face so full of love, so understanding and kind. Every tree, fern and blade of green responded to this iridescent charging, and absorbed it. Then suddenly this resplendent presence moved to another site, as close to me as before, but in a more eastern direction. All the while the nature Angel blessed the myriad growing things, he was smiling. I waited till the presence disappeared beyond my sight. This being was more than a king of devas. In my heart he is the Spirit of the Redwoods."

From Flower's comments it is clear that as tree devas advance, the time comes when they graduate to angelhood. The being she describes in the preceding passage is clearly of that rank. In another setting, she describes an initiatory rite she observed in a forest region between such an Angel and a tree deva. In their kingdom, rites of this kind are far more frequent than in the human line of evolution. The tree deva was standing before an altar–like grotto. Facing it was a great Initiatory Angel reminiscent of an Angel of the Christ Presence. There was a tremendous difference in size between the two beings, the majestic Angel towering over the younger deva. There followed a private exchange between them that was not open to observation. But as this process was taking place, Flower observed the love and profound regard with which the higher presence responded to his companion. Suddenly, there was a great flurry of color, as if the spectrum had been loosened, and she saw hues never before seen. The deva stood immersed in this outpouring, absorbing its bestowal. Then, just as suddenly, all became calm and faded away and there stood the new Angel, tall, glorious, beautiful beyond anything we know on earth.

That was all. But it made Flower wonder how much is going on of a similar holy nature throughout the inner worlds, especially in the depths of forests and on mountain heights. She concluded that if the barriers that separate the human world from God's kingdom could be penetrated, we would all fall on our knees in worshipful awe of the wonders revealed.

Allrays and Allsees

Above the tree devas in the angelic hierarchy are the Angels serving all of nature. Two orders in particular oversee the earth realm. The first of these are the Allrays, also known as Angels of the Heights. Allrays direct affairs of an entire region through their spiritual will. They choose the loftiest peak or highest hilltop from which to ray out their benedictions. It was surely an Allray that Flower saw administering the initiatory rite to the tree deva.

In other encounters with these great nature Angels, Flower observed some of their influences. She recalls a certain trail in a favorite mountain region in southern California. The trail is intersected by three ravinelike watercourses, each one carrying an outpouring from one of three Allrays residing higher up the mountain ridge. The first watercourse had a rose quality, rich in currents of love. The second was emerald green in color, and its currents were strength-giving. The third was turquoise; its waters had a quickening effect that stimulated and benefited the mental body. Flower saw clearly that each of these streams sent forth a river of spiritual power.

Still higher than the Allrays is a glorious order known as the Allsees. Their work, as is so often true of the more advanced Angel ranks, is beyond human comprehension, partly because it is focused on the immediate benefit of the earth rather than of humanity. Flower once observed an Allsee Angel welcoming a group of retreatants who were visiting a mountain citadel for spiritual renewal. But this was unusual, as their work is generally devoted to caring for nature.

Lords of the Mountain

A Mountain Lord Communes
with His Logos

National parks offer many opportunities to draw closer to Angels and nature beings. Not only do they contain some of the finest scenery for the outer eye, but they are often playgrounds for nature's inner inhabitants. Just as one finds different varieties of trees, shrubs, or flowers in different settings, so from one park to another, nature presences differ in their appearance, energy emanation, and service. Flower advises that when we enter a park, we allow our faculties of intuition and inner perception to explore the invisible energies and activities that characterize the area.

One forest will be surcharged with healing radiations which are especially invigorating to the etheric body. Another mountain region will emanate a strong current of reverence for God. Lake country usually attunes us to a feeling of peace; desert, prairie, and other open country quickens our keenness of mind. This contrast in energy frequencies reflects the types of beings ensouling the various territories.

Zion National Park, for example, is ensouled by stately Angels of Power. It is a deva cathedral and radiates waves of positive and strengthening energy. Not many miles away, Bryce Canyon National Park is inhabited by presences that are particularly gentle and loving. Like Yosemite and Yellowstone National Parks, Bryce is a deva playground.

Mountains are centers for immense positive energy and its distribution. As such, they often become the residence of beings known as Lords of the Mountains. To understand the place of these beings in the scheme of things, it is important to realize that the human consciousness can only grasp the simplest beginnings of the glory that the angelic kingdom contains. Its lower reaches include all that has been presented to this point. As one ascends the hierarchy of angelic orders, human knowledge of Angels' nature and rank diminishes, just as the grandeur of the universe overwhelms our capacity to comprehend how God manages its immensity.

Mountain Lords are highly evolved Angels beyond the Allsees. Their work varies from range to range. Some have an initiatory or instructional work to challenge both nature beings and humans to higher accomplishment; others focus on renewal and healing. All such presences are especially committed to the conscious unfoldment of life attracted to their domain.

A mountain region that deeply impressed Flower is Mt. Rainier National Park. It is presided over by a great Lord of the

Mountain. Beams emanating from this magnificent spirit extend far beyond the boundaries of the park, reaching communities and cities some distance away. Upon entering this nature preserve, Flower described hearing the pealing of resonant bells which diminished as she traveled deeper into its interior. She sensed radiations of deepest reverence, almost imperceptible at first, and then increasing in clarity. Gradually, woodland spirits appeared to her, all traveling in the direction of this dominant presence. A mantling of complete devotion and veneration infused the ongoing procession.

Overshadowing the snow-capped dome are the actual head and face of the Lord of Mt. Rainier. He turns slowly in a circle so that he may evenly bless all of the areas of his domain. When the morning dawns, his face turns toward the sunrise. By afternoon he is facing the Paradise Valley region. There are no words in our human language to describe him. To one with inner perception, his expression of serenity and compassion is unforgettable. This particular Lord of the Mountain is as understanding of human beings as he is of the devas in his own kingdom.

It was these encounters with nature shrines that prompted Flower to explore other regions of the United States and the world. She sought to appreciate the vast Angel kingdom serving the earth and especially its power centers around mountains. Time and again, she led groups of her followers to distant places to receive the unique blessings of each nature citadel.

One experience that left a singular impression on her was beholding another Lord of the Mountain at the Matterhorn in Switzerland: "When I stood facing this spiritual giant from my hotel room, I found the presence so overpoweringly awesome that tears rolled down my cheeks. I kept repeating to myself, 'This is what we have come to Europe for—to see you.' All the time we were in Zermatt I felt that the Lord of the Matterhorn's eyes were focused on all individuals within his territory. He looked very benign, yet his presence was almost overwhelming. Seeing him was one of the highest experiences of this lifetime."

Again, years later in a pilgrimage to Mt. Cook in New Zealand, Flower had a similar experience. The location of this mountain on the South Island is rather remote, and its surrounding landscape both pristine and challenging. As she explained, the Lord of this mighty peak is an initiatory being who sees the need to awaken and arouse individuals from their lethargy or self-satisfaction, stirring within them the fires of holy enthusiasm to climb the mountain of God. As Flower explained: "When I first studied Mt. Cook from my room, I was so drawn to the noble Lord of this range that I'm not sure how long I stood there regarding him. When I returned to outer consciousness, my face was wet with tears. Only the Lord of the Matterhorn had touched me as deeply as this all-seeing mountain presence. There are no words to describe his nobility. My inner self wanted to stay on my knees. The outer self wanted to gather the group and tell them what and who was here."

The most advanced of all the mountain Lords reigns from Mt. Everest. From its heights a telepathic network connects with all the high mountains on earth. The intelligences who post themselves on the highest peaks in their respective regions signal each other, back and forth, with blessings and a vital flow of communion.

The journey we have taken through the realm of earth has been brief, with only a sampling of its revelations. Perhaps the most striking impression it leaves behind is the contrast between the outer world of nature, as beautiful as it is, and its inner counterpart, infinitely more wondrous. But beyond the wonder is the unveiling of a kingdom far outnumbering the human population which exists for the sole benefit of nature. Our knowledge of this reality is now awakening from centuries long sleep. We see in the descriptions of seers such as Flower the rediscovery of an invisible world more extraordinary than that revealed by the voyage of Columbus or by Leeuwenhoek and his microscope. With the dawning of the Aquarian Age comes the promise that the humanity of the future will gain the capacity to see through the eye of inner perception this vast dominion of ethereal life.

The Murmlo—Wind Angels Working with Weather

Chapter 4

 *The Realm of Air*

Of the four elements comprising the kingdom of nature, the realm of earth is the most familiar and friendly. The beauty of mountains, deserts, forests, and flower-strewn meadows is firmly imprinted on the consciousness of humankind. Earth is our residence, our safe haven, our principal source of food and shelter, and the gateway to the wonders of the natural landscape.

By contrast, the realm of air is more elusive. Certainly, air is essential to the lives of animals and humans. Moment by moment we breathe in its precious oxygen; it wraps around us in a constant presence, yet it is invisible. We become aware of the air principally when it moves as the wind, and here the true character of the air emerges. Winds can be gentle and caressing, or they can be gusty and capricious. They can be wild and devastating, or they can be altogether still.

Undoubtedly the most obvious manifestation of the element of the air is the weather, since it is at the command of the air currents. Of all the realms of nature, air is the most dangerous and destructive when aroused. Through her clairvoyance Flower has shared with us an important insight into the way in which we can relate to air beings in order to influence the forces shaping weather—especially moderating its extremes. We will come to those observations in a moment.

We can easily lose sight of another function of the air realm. Air is the medium through which sound travels. Beings of this realm are keenly aware of the quality of sounds being generated and transmitted. Anything related to sound is precious to these servers. Though they expect and prefer harmony, beauty, and reverence, it is obvious that most human sounds fall short of this standard—especially noise and profanity. Even the harmless chatter that takes place during large gatherings is sufficiently disturbing so that air intelligences avoid such settings. To live in harmony with the denizens of this sensitive realm, Flower advises that we regard the air as sacred and avoid creating noise or abusive sounds.

Like the realm of earth, the air realm contains a hierarchy of beings ascending from tiny builders to immense and powerful Angels. Air intelligences, by their very nature, exist apart from humans. Like other angelic creatures, air Angels do not approve of our inconstancy toward God's world—our insincerity, indifference, or carelessness. What they respond to most is an attitude of genuine respect and humility. When we practice these qualities keeping the air realm in mind, we earn their respect and appreciation.

How difficult it is for humans to grasp what separates the nature kingdom from our own sense of the world. We struggle to harmonize our higher and lower natures. We accept our imperfections as part of the paradox of being human, experiencing a mixture of good days along with bad. But to an air intelligence, such alteration is irreverent and inexcusable. They know no other purpose, desire, or motive than to serve the Creator, and it makes perfect sense to them that, given free will, the same choice would be ours. Thus, we have much to learn from beings of the air realm. Regardless of their reservations about the inconstancy of our dual natures, they are not spiteful, and they go about their work with joyful eagerness.

Builders, Zephyrs, and Sylphs

The smallest beings in the air realm are called builders. These elementals are minute in size and development; nevertheless, they are resplendent in color and beauty. Their work consists of moving in their etheric forms among flowers, shrubs, and nearly all vegetable life, much like bees gathering pollen, except that their task is facilitating the exchange of carbon dioxide for oxygen. The larger the plant, the more builders it will attract.

Builders Among the Blossoms

Builders are divided into males and females. Their lives extend over a period equivalent to about ten years of earth time. They realize repeated lives of growth in rapid succession. Hardly is life in one body completed than another body more lovely in color and form is prepared for them.

Flower described observing these delicate creatures in the midst of a day: "Infinitely soul-stirring are unexpected glimpses of the nature world at work. Almost resolutely, I daily confine myself to labor at my desk, while outside, little builders are gaily gliding in and above our flower garden. When necessary, however, I steal to the glass doors of our study for a sight of those fairy beings, and the joy that wells up from within as I watch these tiny servers is both relaxing and refreshing."

Many of the imaginary accounts in children's books concerning fairies have their origin in impressions of these little beings, although they are actually much smaller in size than human beings have portrayed. After experiencing some sixty or more changes in bodies as builders, they advance to the next stage of their evolvement. Until this point, their movements have been governed entirely by instinct. They have little understanding of what they do or why, yet their joyousness in being part of an activity that serves as the respiratory system of the nature kingdom gives them boundless fulfillment.

The next youngest form of life in the air realm is known as the zephyr. This being contains the beginnings of active intelligence. When mature, it achieves a height of three feet and possesses a beauty which is seldom paralleled on earth.

How zephyrs come into existence is worthy of note. A zephyr is created by the joyful, playful, adoring ecstasies of its parents. All of nature is composed of pairs of beings opposite in gender. Zephyrs, as parents, fashion their offspring by working together with inspiration. Gestation is not the mother's task alone, as with humans, but a joint enterprise that takes place outside either parent's body. What takes shape resembles an egg rather than an embryo as in human reproduction.

In a moment of ecstatic communion with the lofty intelligences that supervise the air realm, the egglike creation of the two parents opens, and a small, beautiful being emerges— less than a foot tall, but in every other way a replica of its delighted parents. This newly formed zephyr eventually will attain the same height and unfoldment in stature and intelligence as its parents. Its life span ranges from three hundred to five hundred earth years, and its individuality will become strongly apparent as it matures.

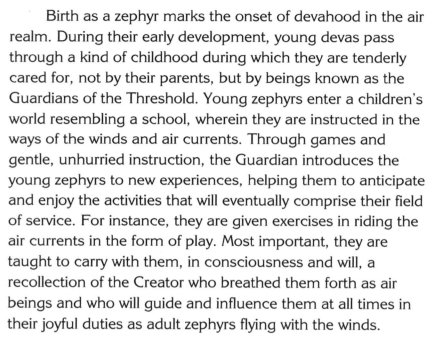

Birth as a zephyr marks the onset of devahood in the air realm. During their early development, young devas pass through a kind of childhood during which they are tenderly cared for, not by their parents, but by beings known as the Guardians of the Threshold. Young zephyrs enter a children's world resembling a school, wherein they are instructed in the ways of the winds and air currents. Through games and gentle, unhurried instruction, the Guardian introduces the young zephyrs to new experiences, helping them to anticipate and enjoy the activities that will eventually comprise their field of service. For instance, they are given exercises in riding the air currents in the form of play. Most important, they are taught to carry with them, in consciousness and will, a recollection of the Creator who breathed them forth as air beings and who will guide and influence them at all times in their joyful duties as adult zephyrs flying with the winds.

While young and still learning to glide upon the air currents, zephyrs take notice of persons, creatures, and places that they will wish to observe more closely later. In a succeeding stage of their growth, when their memory is more reliable and consistent, they will visit the places that once attracted them at a time when they can be of service in bringing about climatic changes needed in these regions.

Mature zephyrs attain a level of intelligence in their etheric bodies equal to an average human. They are devoid of selfish motives springing from personal ambition and deviousness. This freedom from a self-serving will causes them to exceed the possibilities of humans for service at an equal stage of unfoldment.

When very young, zephyrs enjoy riding the air currents most of all. As they grow older, they learn to control air currents and to accelerate or decrease them, especially when winds might become destructive if not altered in velocity. However, an adult zephyr's principal service is deflecting the intensity of the cosmic and solar rays which constantly bombard the earth. To wield a protective influence over the physical world, especially those specific regions that they have come to love and inhabit, zephyrs concentrate their efforts on the etheric level to normalize overcharged cosmic forces that otherwise threaten the earth. As they subdue these intensifications of energy, zephyrs' bodies change color temporarily. Sometimes when they are receiving a celestial bombardment, zephyrs become shimmering creatures, brilliant and crystalline in appearance. Often they will be seen to take on a sapphire hue or, when releasing certain solar overchargings, vivid tones of yellow-orange. These transformations are short-lived, perhaps no more than twenty-four earth hours, long enough for the excess charges to be safely disposed of.

It is wise for us to realize that zephyrs, which move about us in gentle and playful breezes, are busy beyond our comprehension. Moreover, as is true of the other beings of the angelic realm, we should recognize and appreciate their selfless enterprise in serving their Creator.

Above the zephyrs are the sylphs, who are older, wiser, and more developed citizens of the air realm. Were you to have the good fortune to behold this form of life, sylphs would appear to be swimming through the atmosphere. Sylphs are air devas whose bodies, when upright, greatly resemble human beings in stature, averaging between three and five feet in height. Like all those of deva origin, they exist in their etheric bodies for at least five hundred earth years. Sylphs, though not as yet Angels, are far more intuitive than even the most developed spiritual seekers among humankind. What also sets them apart from humans is their instantaneous and wholehearted obedience to their superiors.

The work of sylphs is similar to that of zephyrs, though more powerful. Into the etheric envelope of earth's atmosphere come literally hundreds of rays, mostly of solar origin. Sylphs work with etheric conditions created by these solar and cosmic forces. They are unable to prevent the accumulated radiations of these beams, but they can create spacious energy canopies of sufficient size to act as screens to reduce the force of the penetrating rays. Depending on the needs of a tree, a hillside, a mountain, or a community, sylphs work individually or as a group to build beautiful screens fashioned from their own etheric substances. These canopies enhance the mixture of natural energies to benefit each particular region and its purpose.

The Angels of the Winds

When air devas take their next upward step they enter the ranks of angelhood, becoming Angels of the Winds, or Cilarae. Their task is to manage the steadfast air currents caused by the earth's rotation. These currents include prevailing westerly winds, equatorial winds, and other winds whose names are familiar in their own locales. Since air currents are in constant motion, they are like rivers of air. Depending on their individual preferences, Cilarae are drawn to particular regions of the atmosphere. There they serve as faithful sentinels watching over the unceasing streams of air.

According to their development, Cilarae range in size from eight to ten feet when standing upright. This, however, is not their usual posture, for they are most often observed in a swimming or diving position moving through the air rivers they supervise. At times they will travel in this manner three thousand miles or more to reach a destination. When their mission is complete, most of these wind beings return to their home region for renewal and repose.

Related to the Cilarae are the Murmlo, a group of Angels which frequent coastal areas, influencing the coming of storms or welcoming changes in the weather. The word *murmur* is related to these steadfast servers of the seas and oceans of air. Murmlo are equal in advancement to Cilarae, but theirs is a different kind of service. Sometimes they work for periods equivalent to several days to bring about needed changes in the weather. They do this by interacting with the forces that underlie air pressures and temperatures in the regions they frequent. If wholly natural conditions are not sufficient to induce storms, the Murmlo, like sylphs, create gigantic energy structures in the etheric plane which resemble the clouds of the physical world. These etheric formations alter the prevailing air pressure to generate a storm. As long as no violent or destructive forces are created in the atmosphere, the Murmlo can use their knowledge of air currents to bring about desired weather changes.

The Murmlo and Cilarae Angels are in charge of younger orders of nature beings, including zephyrs and sylphs. However, during serious storms, these younger beings are sent out of the disturbed territories, leaving advanced Angels to deal with the more severe weather elements.

Flower taught that climatic havoc is created on earth not by the Angels of the nature kingdom, but by negative feelings and thoughts which arise from humanity's capacity for violence, cruelty, and perversion. Violent forces gravitate toward vicinities in which antisocial or otherwise unskillful actions take place. As negative etheric energies build up over time, they become so massive and contain such smoldering violence that their pent-up fury must be released or defused from time to time. Otherwise, the planet could not sustain human life.

Tornados and hurricanes are, thus, a necessary venting of these explosive accumulations. Whenever a catastrophe occurs on the physical plane, such as an earthquake, a cyclonic storm, or a similar destructive disturbance, nature intelligences have been offended by the sacrilege of irreverent human beings. Angels do not allow such storms to occur from an attitude of punishment or retaliation; nor are they the cause of such dis-asters. They simply allow areas to be cleansed of the malevolent energies that have accumulated in them so that the whole planet will not suffer destruction. If, in a certain area, there is a danger of a tornado, Flower warned us, its citizens would do well to pur-ify themselves of selfishness, deceitfulness, and hatred. Hurri-canes, in a like manner, result from a buildup in the inhabitants of a region of the etheric products of bad temper, prejudices, and greed.

Like disturbances of the air, floods follow from the emotional instability, prejudice, and hatred of people in particular vicinities. Floods occur despite precautions taken because the accumulation of negative emotions demands an outlet. To conquer floods from the standpoint of their inner

causation, Flower taught that we must change the consciousness of people, freeing them from race hatred and from
harmful pettiness and bickering. When humankind is watchful
of its destructive emotions, rivers will flow serenely without
damaging the areas through which they move.

Airwee, Electric Angels, and Other Angels of Air

All the angelic presences serving to influence the
atmosphere and weather—a vast domain encompassing most
of the air realm—come under the order of the Airwee. The
Angels of this type are in charge of deciding upon and governing atmospheric conditions. For example, so-called Electric
Angels deal with magnetism and the forces of electricity. If the
earth is lacking certain elements or the etheric or lower astral
planes are heavy with impurities, these beings see to it that
lightning is attracted. In time, when humanity's consciousness
is more uniformly developed, we will have much to learn from
the Electric Angels about the harnessing and control of this
powerful element.

If rain, snow or fog are needed, the Airwee set into motion
the forces of the Murmlo along with the Neentel who, together,
arrange the conditions necessary for making a storm. The
Neentel, one of the smaller groups of the Airwee order, control
weather rhythms in particular seasons. Within these rhythms
such things as the patterns of snowflakes and frost are formed.

An Electric Angel

Flower described this encounter with a magnificent Airwee at Questhaven: "One evening a walk was lengthened so that I might observe a being of considerable size who proved to be a director of Weather Angels. The communication between this superior and his charge was lost to me, but with the nature devas he addressed, my higher sensibilities were quickened by this great one's appearance."

While the Airwee comprise the general body of intelligences serving the air realm, their locus of activity is within the earth's atmosphere. The stratosphere, on the other hand, is the dwelling place of the highest and most exalted order of air intelligences. Their islands of space are immense, and their sanctuaries of infinite peace are beyond human comprehension. One group of beings of this type are the Tija. They are tremendously advanced, masterly, and lordly presences of both genders. All decisions as to changes in climate, rainfall, and the fertility of earth are considered by the Tija and implemented under their guidance. Some of their rank serve the water realm, as well. Most Tija are Archangels or higher.

Appeals to the Weather Angels

While the realm of earth is the most friendly where humans are concerned, the air is most dangerous. Its intelligences demand constancy, fidelity, humility, and appreciation—qualities that, among humankind, sometimes seem to be in short supply. Notice, for example, that a strong wind can sometimes make one feel uneasy. When the elementals of air are adversely aroused by accumulations of humanity's disrespect and arrogance, their response can be fierce and unforgiving. At the other extreme, the absence of winds when they are needed can be equally disconcerting. A dead calm on a hot summer's day, or the cessation of winds about the equator called the doldrums, often doomed entire crews in the days of sailing vessels. This is not to say that air beings are themselves malevolent, but their intolerance of the downside of human nature can make them a volatile force to be reckoned with. To address this challenge, wise individuals should not take the nature kingdom or any of its realms for granted.

Knowledge of the various orders that serve the medium of air can also help us direct our prayer work. If a particular region has need of rain, we should pray to the Murmlo to activate changes in the winds to bring rain clouds into the stricken area. If we are flying and want to ensure our safety among the air currents, we can pray to the Cilarae for a smooth flight. If we are concerned about a diminishing ozone layer, we might direct our prayers to the steadfast air sylphs asking them to prepare protective screens. Air intelligences are ever watchful of how humans regard their domain. If we are indifferent to the sources of pollution or other air contamination or are actually among the abusers, we invite disaster. On the other hand, if we are conscious of this peril and vigilant in its prevention, these same intelligences will be deeply appreciative.

In Chapter Three we spoke about mountains and their place in the earth realm. Mountains are also the dwelling place of air beings such as the Airwee. Remember the old adage, "Mountains make their own weather"? In the heights of mountain ranges, winds are irresistibly drawn to ascend and descend their rugged slopes. They find exhilaration and renewal in this vertical environment. Mt. Everest and indeed the entire Himalayan range is the planetary headquarters for the beings of the air realm, as well as their favorite playground.

The realm of air also carries with it a significance beyond the earth's atmosphere. It symbolizes consciousness—that part of us that has the ability to soar into the heights of enlightenment and revelation. Just as it is vital to preserve the purity of the air we breathe, so is it vital to preserve the purity of the thoughts and feelings that constitute consciousness. Our consciousness is the air realm within. All of nature, and the beings of the air realm in particular, expect us to exhibit self-mastery. The survival of the human race testifies to nature's patience, which has provided us with many second chances to prove ourselves worthy of coexisting with her. It follows that as we become aware of the inhabitants and ways of her kingdom, we become exemplars of the respect and appreciation she deserves, indeed, role models of conduct for all of humanity.

A Garden Deva in Reverent Attunement

Chapter 5

 The Realm of Water

Human history is richly interwoven with stories of the sea. Mythology, with its tales of water sprites, sea nymphs, mermaids, and the Sirens of Homer's Odyssey, testifies to humanity's fascination with the realm of water and its population. While the legends were often based on fanciful speculation, the existence of water intelligences unmistakably shines through the classic tales.

Water covers three-quarters of the earth's surface and is the primary constituent of the human body itself. As the basic building block that underlies the design of life, water supports the most numerous and vivid population of superphysical beings. Of the four realms, water beings are the most emotional and changeable. Indeed, they are synonymous with the world of emotions, making them dynamic, colorful, and excitable in temperament. A person with inner perception sees their excitable nature in fast-moving rivers and streams. This reaches a climax in cascades and waterfalls. To live in harmony with these beings, humans must work to understand and appreciate their many moods and expressions.

Oceanids and Water Sprites

The youngest spiritual forms to be found in the water realm are called oceanids, so named because of their source. These elementals are no larger than the drops of water they ensoul. Their work is to purify and energize the units of water which come into their sphere of activity. As they are ready for more distinctive service, the Angels of the water world who work with the principle of evaporation lift worthy oceanids up into the atmosphere and deposit them through rains in areas where they are needed. After a time the migrating oceanids are again drawn into the vicinity of springs, streams, or rivers. Or, by the principle of percolation, they become part of the underground rivers and lakes upon which the earth's wells and reservoirs depend.

If, during a rain storm, oceanids happen to fall directly into a stream or river, they will remain with that body of water for most of their lives. Their work at this stage of their evolution is to help blend the elements into the common mixture of substances comprising water in any given location. The oceanid existence is instinctive and unconscious yet full of pleasure and purposefulness.

It is important to keep in mind that what meets our outer eye when we look at nature is often only a part of the story. Certainly, the cycle of water evaporation and condensation, so familiar to us from our school days, is missing the vital superphysical element of the process as Flower described it. Without her extended viewpoint, we are left with a strictly mechanical picture involving only such variables as temperature and atmospheric conditions. Revealed for what they are, all natural processes, including those of the water realm, are seen as inspirited by a world of living entities behind the scenes who provide the true energy and direction which we experience as the nature kingdom.

When they have completed their service as elementals, tiny oceanids evolve to another young stage of existence as water sprites. The delightful company of creatures that six-year-old Flower saw skimming across the water of New York harbor were undoubtedly beings of this type. The transform-ation from oceanid to water sprite is considerable, as the former is the size of a water drop and the latter is about eight inches high. Water sprites are, as yet, unaware of their individual purpose in the scheme of things, though they are instrumental in serving the upward slope of the planet's evolution. Obedient to their endowments and the directives of their superiors, sprites ride the waters of their domain gleefully, rejoicing that they are traveling to the sea, the home of their origin.

Sea Nymphs and Naiads

Water beings in great numbers also dwell beneath the surface of the earth. They attend the waters which constitute our water tables, underground lakes and rivers, and the source of our springs. Their assignment is, in part, a sacrificial condition for their unfoldment. What a moment of glory it is to these intelligences, regardless of their stage of evolution, to be able to come to the surface of the earth through whatever outlets afford this opportunity! Imagine the exhilaration any human would feel, after years of confinement in a dark cave deep underground, to be brought once again into the sunlight. A similar joy brightens the countenances of those serving the water world.

As water beings move upward in their stages of growth, not only does their height and strength increase, but so do their intuitional capacities and their responsiveness to the lofty Tija who is in charge of their unfoldment. Above the water sprite in advancement is the sea nymph, comparable in intelligence and capabilities to the gnomes of the earth realm. Sea nymphs are generally from eighteen to twenty-four inches high. The pictures humans have drawn of these creatures are generally accurate, especially of the upper portion of their bodies. However, contrary to imaginative claims, sea nymphs do not possess a fish–like torso or lower body. Instead, they have human-shaped feet which are usually in a swimming position, for, like their counterparts who ride the air streams, sea nymphs spend their lives riding the surface currents of moving bodies of water.

Above the sea nymphs in angelic evolution are the naiads, who range up to three feet in stature. They are more intelligent and their experience is richer and more distinctive than their forerunners among water creatures. Naiads are the first water forms who serve with conscious volition, a significant milestone in advancement. Their preference is to attend bodies of fresh water, though their specific locale changes constantly, because it is unusual for any water intelligence below the stage of angelhood to be permitted to serve in one place for more than a season.

Also with the naiad stage comes the beginning recognition that waters are to be cleared, that each river has a unique destiny, and that the will of the river king needs to be carried out in minute detail. These responsible and wide-ranging realizations show naiads to be equivalent to the tree devas in the earth realm. The river king, whom the naiads serve, is an advanced being under whose charge are the flowing rivers of the world.

Angels of the Waters

An Angel of the Falls

Above the devas of the waters are its Angels. Nereids are water Angels who serve in many capacities. Beautifully tall, Nereids reflect the shimmering moon colors which are natural to the water world. Nereids of the feminine gender predominate as supervising Angels in underground caverns. This is true also on the surface of the earth, where quiet bodies of water, like ponds or lakes, and waterfalls of modest height are generally attended by feminine Nereids. However, bodies of moving water, such as major rivers and waterfalls, are usually under the care of a Nereid who is masculine in polarity and service.

Flower observed one such glorious water Angel while visiting Snoqualmie Falls in the state of Washington. He stood as tall as the height of the falls and sent forth emanations that consecrated the surrounding area. Flower noticed that as the younger water elementals passed through the resplendent aura of this advanced presence, they visibly gained a surcharge of renewal.

The Realm of Water

The Nereids of lakes, particularly those of advanced development, are prompted to expand the aura of the waters they oversee to the greatest distance possible. This same activity holds true for the oceans, where the Nereids serving the Pacific Ocean extend its aura all the way to the Rocky Mountains. The aura of the Atlantic Ocean touches the eastern slopes of the same great mountain chain. This endeavor consumes the energies of countless angelic lives, which are dedicated to tireless work to expand the purifying auras of bodies of water.

In addition to being entrusted with more comprehensive and advanced service, the Nereids and other Angels of the water are different from the less evolved beings of the realm in another way. Until angelhood dawns, the lives of water beings are characterized by much friction, excitability, and instability. Indeed, of all the realms, the water world has the strongest rivalry between rivers, lakes, and even between the great oceans. This is due, in part, to the link between water and the emotions. However, at the level of Nereids and above, water intelligences exhibit an attitude of inclusiveness and whole-heartedness which is natural to the beings of the other three realms at an earlier phase of development.

A vast company of water beings and Angels serve the oceans of the world, with countless multitudes of all the types thus far mentioned. Their united labor is to purify and recharge the ocean waters and to work with their counterparts in the air realm to accomplish the perpetual cycle that moves water from sea to land and back to the sea again. Angels of the sea can best be seen at night. They possess shimmering auras which reminded Flower of a robe with light blue and apple green

tones. Once when she was traveling to Europe by boat, Flower went out on the deck and saw a huge round face come up out of the waves which was like nothing she had ever seen before. She was told by the Guardian Angel who was always her teacher that it was an Angel interested in the higher forms of sea life, such as dolphins.

Angel of the Sea with Dolphins

Each of the immense bodies of water on earth is ruled by an extra-ordinary Angel who has earned the title of Sea Lord. The Pacific Ocean has such an august presence. He is peaceful, powerful, and wondrously influential. His name in the inner worlds is Pericos. The Atlantic Ocean possesses a Sea Lord of comparable attainment whose name is Ceranus. The Indian Ocean, the Mediterranean Sea, and all bodies of water known by distinctive names are watched over by such noble intelligences.

The existence of these Angelic Lords is reflected in the stories told in Greek and Roman mythology about Poseidon or Neptune, ruler of the ocean depths. As the myths also hint, each Ocean Lord oversees an infinite network of evolving servers, who work in their various regions to maintain the principles of evaporation, transpiration, and percolation upon which the watery body of our planet so vitally depends.

The supreme head of the water world is a lofty Tija, or Angel Prince. With the counsel of higher angelic beings, he makes decisions about the mingling of water and wind to bring about needed changes in climate. Most of what a Tija does is beyond human understanding. Still, it is helpful to be aware of his existence and mindful of the ascending hierarchy of angelic orders which characterizes superphysical life in each of the realms of nature.

Interacting with the Beings of the Waters

The world of water is easily taken for granted by humankind, but without water, the earth would be a barren desert. Water softens the land and prepares it to bring forth food. Moreover, as we have noted, water is the nearest natural equivalent to human emotion. As such, the water realm is made up of intelligences that are normally friendly to humans. Yet, as with all the other realms, much depends on our outlook and manner. If we are insensitive and careless in our treatment of water, we will not be well received by the beings of this element. Since human emotions are the basis of our similarity with the inhabitants of the water realm, we must act with emotional self-control if we wish to interact fruitfully with its intelligences.

When we are involved with water, either traveling on its surface or swimming, we are wise to exercise control over our thoughts and feelings, even our manner of speaking and movement. It may seem strange that the medium of water, which is itself unstable and excitable, should be the most demanding of us in this respect. Yet, it is often the case in the psychology of temperaments that one is most sensitive to annoying qualities in others that remind us of our own problematic tendencies. Thus it should not be surprising that the intelligences of the water realm react strongly to our unruly emotions. What is more remarkable is that humans have so much in common with the superphysical beings of this realm.

This similarity gives water many beneficial properties. One of water's principal gifts to us is its ability to cleanse the etheric body. When we bathe or take a shower, our aura is purified of the negative magnetism that accumulates there. For at least four hours after bathing, one's aura will be free of this buildup, which often appears as a gray film to those who possess inner sight.

When we are in the presence of an ocean or a great waterfall, the aura, especially the aura of our etheric body, dissolves, becoming liquid and waterlike. The outlines of the aura, which were previously quite definite, become protean and take on the appearance of the energies emanating from the water source. Something similar, though usually less pronounced, happens when one encounters rivers or lakes. Oceans have unique abilities to cleanse the etheric body. But for some individuals, especially those who are spiritually sensitive, there comes a point when the cleansing of the etheric body has gone on long enough. For such a person, continuing in an ocean atmosphere can lead to depleting one's energy. A long sea voyage might seem beneficial emotionally and mentally, but it may not always be beneficial to one's energy body.

Another attribute of water works on our emotions. Bodies of water that are normally peaceful and calm, such as oceans, lakes, and ponds, are home to elementals who help us to relax and come to peace. The elementals associated with rivers and streams are more active and stimulating in their effects, arousing similar energies in us. The emotional effect of being near fast-moving water can be invigorating or can cause us to feel restless and nervous.

As Flower describes it, our bodies project an aura which reflects, in particular, our physical, etheric, emotional, and mental states of being. The atoms that comprise each of these energy fields, especially the emotional aspect of the aura, are sensitive to outside influences. Around bodies of water that are fast moving and excitable, the water beings giving rise to these emotions project thought forms that are themselves excited. These tend to scatter and disperse, eventually entering the auras of humans in their vicinity. The result, while varying with individuals, is a mirroring of these emotional reactions. When we are overcharged with excess energy, water beings can also affect us in the other direction, and being near quiet lakes or peaceful oceans can help us relax and release tensions.

Another benefit of water is that it can encourage clear self-examination. Water's emotional qualities prompt us to look at the state of our own consciousness. Is our state of mind tranquil and calm like a still lake at evening or is it active and busy like a swiftly running river? If we find evidence of an imbalance of agitation, forcefulness, or aggressiveness, water can remind us to seek for self-command and control. More-over, the easy flow of water symbolizes the outflowing of spiritualized love, which the water elementals expect from us. In receiving our love, these tireless beings are further inspired to work tirelessly for humanity and its good.

The last great blessing of the water world is its purifying properties. As we drink in the goodness of water, we can give thanks for its ability to remove from our bodies all manner of dross. When we bathe, we can give thanks again for bodies which are refreshed and rinsed free of dust and grime. Water rids us of all impurities physically and stands ready to do the same for our hearts and minds. It is one of life's paradoxes that the two great purifiers on the planet earth are water and fire—two elements that are opposites and that consume each other. And it is to the world of fire we now turn.

A Lord of Flame

Chapter 6

 The Realm of Fire

The mysterious realm of fire is the most evolved of the four realms, the most evanescent, and the one least experienced consciously. In spite of its mystery or, indeed, because of it, fire assumes a significant role in our ceremonies. Spiritual traditions around the world use candles in holy observances—to commemorate the dead, celebrate consecration rites, and mark all manner of significant spiritual passages. In everyday life, we light candles to symbolize our prayers and wishes, to celebrate birthdays and anniversaries, and to create a festive or contemplative mood. In ancient times sacred fires were kept burning perpetually as a sign of a holy order's link with the Divine, and the hearth of a home was regarded as a place of consecration.

Fire is fascinating because it is the source of light, and light is what connects us with God. Fire is at once the flame of aspiration, the burning of holy enthusiasm, the warmth of spiritual ardor, and the sunburst of illumination. Of the four elements, fire stirs us most deeply and holds the most promise for opening the gates of inner perception. For the most part, the angelic hosts of the fire realm have little to do with humankind until individuals have experienced illumination itself—that transforming moment when their eyes are opened to the kingdom of God within, and they set forth on the great quest for enlightenment. Such an experience often begins as an inner fire, and once ignited, it burns as a celestial desire to fathom life's meaning and purpose. It is an awakening common to all spiritual paths. Yet, at the same time, in the short history of human evolution, it remains an uncommon occurrence, making its recipients exceptional.

The element of fire, then, is closely linked to the advent of spiritual enlightenment. As such, it requires of us integrity, earnestness, enthusiasm, and holy desire. Until these qualities are present, we are outside the territory which is under the watchful eyes of fire beings. Once they are active, and our praying and visualization become more earnest, we attract representatives of the fire realm. They, in turn, help us to think and speak in ways that bring about spiritual growth.

But we are getting ahead of our story. Before we consider the luminous Angels of fire, we look first at the realm's younger inhabitants.

Fire Elementals, Salamanders, and Flamin

Salamander

Fire beings below the rank of angelhood have very little interest in or involvement with humans. These entities, ranging from elementals to devas, are present wherever fire is found. The youngest of the elementals appear as fire specks and are no larger than snowflakes, which they resemble. Whenever we light a match we create sparks or a flame that for a brief moment brings these fire elementals visibly into the physical dimension from their invisible etheric world.

Next to these in order come salamanders who vary in height from eight inches to as much as two feet. Flower has reported that their faces are always seen in the tongue of the flame and that most have very long, thin features. Their faces, moreover, reveal a lively intensity which is apparent in their eyes as well as in the spirited movements with which they tend the flames. Salamanders lack any desire to interact with humans; in fact, they are not even aware that we exist. They are totally absorbed in their singular mission, which is to purify the environment of accumulated deadwood and debris—to use it up and extinguish all refuse.

The next stage of growth for these young beings is as flamin, who range in stature from two to eight feet, depending on the size of the conflagration which they inhabit. Possessing limited intelligence, but having no soul consciousness as yet, flamin are particularly instinctive and focused in their endeavors. Their work is to simplify, purify, and cleanse physically and psychically the buildup of debris that can be the cause of potentially destructive fires.

We must remember that forests are put at risk primarily by human carelessness, especially when aggravated by a wanton disregard for the well-being of the natural environment. This tendency is further complicated by a kind of morbid fascination some persons have in witnessing the awesome power of fire to consume whatever is in its path. In spite of these aberrations, fire is for the most part a welcome and constructive element on our planet, and one that, as is explained below, holds great spiritual significance.

Fanning the Fires of Spiritual Aspiration

Above the flamin in the world of fire are intelligences which govern, stimulate, and regenerate the lives of humans, Angels, and other forms of creation. The one purpose of the Fire Angels is to ignite and sustain the fires of spirituality wherever fuel for this transforming energy is found.

Baptism of the Amfri

Although, as has been noted, most of the great intelligences of the fire realm have little or nothing to do with people, the Amfri are fire Angels who work deeply with human beings. Their work is accelerating the spiritual evolution of all they touch.

The Amfri are tall, glowing, exceedingly beautiful, fiery presences who work primarily through the mental dimension. They steadfastly seek out persons in earthly bodies with strong desire to reach toward the light, watching constantly for the fires of spiritual aspiration to rise from these devotees. Many human seekers are firelike for only brief periods. The Amfri witness the auric fires which momentarily flash from such individuals.

In those moments, when the body and faculties are united in spiritual ardor, the Amfri have the opportunity to enter into more direct contact with humans. They hover over these souls with a love similar to that of Guardian Angels, with whom they are comparable in unfoldment, and strive to cleanse aspirants of the dross which weighs them down, hardens them, and separates them from God-Light. With help from the Divine Source, through the fire of spiritual incentives, human seekers burning with holy fire are impregnated with an activated sense of oneness with God, a unifying experience that can be life changing.

Amfri are also involved in the working out of karma. When we meet karmic lessons, three kinds of Angels gather to assist us: Guardian Angels, Karmic Angels, and the Amfri. They study our reactions and send us promptings and impressions aimed at concluding the lesson constructively. The Amfri are especially interested in the purification of human emotions, since their work includes the transmutation of feelings.

Again, this process is a matter of an individual's receptivity. If we can get our personal prejudices and mistaken preconceptions out of the way and open up our consciousness to fresh currents of realization, then Angels such as these can penetrate our normal barricades of self-will. They are then free to drop into our minds, out-of-the-blue so to speak, insights and recognitions that remove the scales from our eyes and illuminate our thought processes. This is accomplished by an exchange between the energy fields of the auras of the Angel and the human, analogous to the transmission of radio waves.

In this connection, the Amfri are also responsible for the perfecting of human relationships. Their very essence is love.

Flower and other teachers have revealed to us that love, beauty, reverence, and courage are all in essence flame–like. When these qualities energize the whole being, relationships, tasks, plans, and worship come together in an inner fire which energizes, purifies, and transforms us at the deepest level.

In such moments, humans are spiritually at one with the great fire beings who offer them liberation from their imprisonment in matter. When aspirants achieve a spiritual constancy, their sense of reverence resembles flamelike aureoles burning brightly in their auras. Once this state is achieved, new outbreaks of divine conflagration ignite constantly to brighten the fiery powers of their receptivity. The flamelike auras of spiritual desire serve as well to keep seekers constantly under the surveillance of the magnificent Angels of Fire.

When a human being experiences initiation, the Amfri responsible for the unfoldment of his or her soul makes spiritual contact with the next higher angelic order. These higher fire beings are the Firl, who are channels for the flow of electrical baptism. Firl are more highly developed than Amfri and exist only in the causal or soul world. Firl come into active play when an individual's whole being yearns for purity, dependability, and fidelity to light. Working on the soul level, they manipulate electrical properties to further the unfoldment of men and women who are ready and receptive. For their part, Amfri Angels await opportunities to condition individuals, both in consciousness and in auric radiation, to withstand the electrical supercharging which accompanies all major spiritual initiations. Thus, whereas an Amfri concentrates on extinguishing the dross in a human's charge by consuming it in soul fires lit from within, a Firl's specific duty is to wield an electric baptism of causal energies that penetrates the higher bodies of the candidate for the purpose of initiation and its coincident illumination.

It is worth noting how many beings and intelligences contribute to one soul's rebirth. For each human being who is prepared for the gateway to enlightenment, as many as seven or more close associates in the human line have been actively interested in this person's advancement. On the angelic side, an equal number of lofty intelligences contribute to a human's enlightenment. Besides the Guardian Angels, the Karmic Angels, and the Amfri Angels mentioned previously, the Firl, angelic representatives of the Lord Christ and the Holy Spirit and, depending on the candidate, other angelic presences may be involved. Together, and at the proper moment, the angelic host make possible a grounding of solar beams which permanently transform the consciousness and habit patterns of the human being whom they touch.

Flower tells of an experience she had during an Easter sunrise in the early years of Questhaven. As on all such occasions, she would observe on the horizon tremendous Solar Angels. But on this particular Easter an extraordinary thing happened. Great Solar Angels appeared in the sky, as before, creating an intense light. Then, suddenly, out of this fiery brilliance she beheld the Lord Christ. He addressed a brief prayer to the one He called Father and, at its conclusion, the light grew in intensity and, with it, the forms of the Christ and the great Solar Angels grew a hundredfold. As they disappeared into the light, she heard a voice coming from a great height, sounding like deep bell tones, saying: "with greater power I thee imbue." The baptism of this blessing remained with Flower for weeks and was one of her most precious memories.

In addition to their esoteric duties, the Firl can render us a very practical service. They are the Angels to whom we can address prayers for fire protection. During fire-endangered seasons or situations, we should mention the Firl by name. Not only are these Angels of sufficient advancement to intervene effectively, but they have a caring and constructive regard for humans, as well as for the entire planet's wholesome evolution.

The Solar Logos and Angels of the Morning and Evening

Above the Firl are the Pitris, who are known in the inner worlds as the Fathers of Fire. These lordly, fiery ones have little to do with human states or experiences. Their cardinal function is to serve as linking bridges of planetary connection under the direct supervision of the Solar Logos, who is the Supreme Fire Being of this planetary system. The hierarchy of fire is vast and complicated, with numerous stages of beings beyond the Petris leading up toward God the Creator and numerous stages below the Amfri leading down to the young fire beings who by their ensoulment make possible the conditions under which fire appears in the earthly realm.

As the Supreme Being of the fire realm, the Solar Logos has as a most visible and powerful symbol the sun itself. It is clear why ancient people worshiped the sun. Beyond its obvious gifts of light and warmth, it is the source of immense spiritual radiations that far exceed its physical dispensations. A multitude of angelic hosts serve the magnificent Solar Logos. Those whose effects are most visible to human eyes are the glorious Angels of the Morning and Evening.

Angels of the Morning are the creators of one of the earth's most magnificent displays, the sunrise. No two sunrises are exactly the same, and for those of us who make the effort to experience it, each sunrise is a magical moment which all of nature awaits with hushed expectancy. The Angels of the Morning are resplendent artisans who fashion an infinite sequence of sunrises to celebrate the eternal and inexhaustible wonders of God's handiwork. They add to the beauty of these moments tones of celestial music along with gentle healing currents which they are uniquely capable of transmitting. Morning Angels always precede the sun's rays over the earth's horizon, and their effect on all of humanity and, for that matter, all of life is one of quickening our love and sense of thanks-giving.

High noon is another significant time of dispensation from the Solar Logos. Viewed from the inner planes, the Logos' dispersion of light causes the etheric world to glow with saffron-colored luminescent beams, whereas in the astral world the radiations are a lucid larkspur blue. This variation of color tones is meaningful. Beings from the nature kingdom who work on the etheric levels require the rhythmic stimulation of the Logos, whose force reaches them as a flame-colored wave of shimmering light. This charging serves both as an internal purification and as a stimulant, acting to absorb the accumu-lated etheric matter which fills the auras of the builders.

The noontide rays also have irresistible influence upon our own etheric bodies. We sense it as a glowing of our energy body and are often aware of an afterglow for an indefinite period. These sensations are most perceptible when we are outdoors in the sunlight. The sun gives our outer and inner bodies a vital keenness that comes in no other way. In these times of the atmosphere's depleted ozone layer, we must take ,of the sun's life-giving rays every day, however briefly.

Angels of the Evening are no less skilled than their morning companions in the creation of splendor. The energy they radiate, however, is much more peaceful. Whereas the incentive of the morning is awaken and rededicate, the message of the evening is rest and reflect. One with inner vision can sense that at sunset, we are quietly studied by the higher intelligences associated with the sun, so that they can better appraise our capacities and readiness for new ascents of the mountain of spiritual development.

Christmas Angels of Fire

The fire realm has an especially significant connection to the coming of Christmas. During Advent, the earth's atmosphere is surcharged by fire beings. From these beings flow the fervency and the ecstasy which, in its weakest aspect, is experienced as responsive feeling and, at its most intense, attainment of the sublimity of exaltation. The highest frequencies of light which flood the atmosphere during this charged time are channeled through fire beings who are pure beyond human capacity to realize their nature.

All sources of divine creation contribute to the life waves which encourage growth, attainment of beauty, and purity of spirit. But it is from the Angels of Fire that a force of encouragement flows which relates humanity directly to the Divine Source. Especially on Christmas Eve, the Angels of Fire help us to remember that heavenly hosts more advanced than the Petris exist in the universe, whose hosannas are dynamic empowerings, and whose mighty radiations brighten and enlighten all dimensions.

In the Church of the Holy Quest at Questhaven Retreat, a candle lighting service at Christmastime is a most holy ritual. Flower has described the presence of great Angels at this ceremony, including those from the fire realm. Flames of aspiration are ignited from these beings in the auras of the congregation as they make their vows to Christ and light their individual candles. One participant described how, at that transcendent moment when his gift to his Lord was the conquest of a long entrenched and destructive habit, he felt consumed in flames as if he himself were the candle. Flower later commented that an Amfri Angel had ensouled this person to ensure that his resolve would be lasting.

The Benediction of a Budiel Angel

Chapter 7

Angels and the Animal Kingdom

We have now looked at the the Angels of the nature wave who serve life on earth through the four elements of earth, air, water, and fire. When we think of nature, however, we also think of the animal kingdom, a realm with a unique relationship to human beings. This important part of the natural world is served by the Angels of the life motivation wave, one of the four main branches of Angels serving life on earth mentioned in Chapter 1.

Aqui, Folatel, and Budiel

The three orders of Angels who work with animals each concentrate on a different aspect of an animal's well-being, support, or supervision. The most unfolded order of Angels serving the animals is the Aqui. This order is composed of two subdivisions, the Folatel and the Budiel.

Folatel Angels are charged with caring for the physical well-being of animals. They employ bands of energy that guide the behavior of the creatures in their care who have yet to develop active mental bodies. In this manner, the Folatel Angels provide the governing influence which we know as instincts that motivate the animal to locate food and shelter, produce offspring, protect and defend against danger, and care for itself when it is ill or injured.

This care is extended to all creatures, including such commonplace and unappreciated species as rodents and reptiles. The Folatel Angel entrusted with the responsibility for such species stimulates a rapid sequence of births and deaths, which, in the long run, move lower animals along their unfoldment to more refined and constructive forms of life. This striving for unfoldment underlies all of creation and is the driving force behind evolution itself.

Budiel Angels also work with creatures at all levels of development. Their work is to guide the progress and growth of individual characteristics among the animals under their care. This function is similar to that provided to humans by Angels of Destiny. Budiel Angels are especially watchful for any signs of emerging individuality. Such tendencies begin to appear as an animal nears the threshold of domestication. Individual traits in animals are highly prized by these Angels, who are very nurturing toward and protective of such promising trends, because they mark the end of the animal's complete dependence on instincts and the beginning of intelligence and choice.

Above the Folatel and the Budiel Angels are the Aqui Angels themselves, transcendent beings who not only supervise the two lower orders but who are in charge of preparing animals for higher stages of advancement. The Aqui work with animals who are at the threshold of graduating from the animal kingdom itself, often to become nature intelligences such as those we have been considering. Others are being prepared for evolution to an advanced form of life elsewhere in the universe. The depth of feeling and outreach to animals shown by human beings plays a vital role in helping animals at the point of transition cross over this evolutionary threshold.

Devas of the Swimmers and Flyers

The Folatel and Budiel Angels exist in a hierarchy of development. In the lower ranks of the Folatel order are devas who are being trained for angelhood. They serve, for example, as the caretakers of sea life, from which all mammals originally evolved. One such group of beings is the pentee devas, who regulate the fixed habits and cyclic experiences of fish. A second group, more advanced, are the twan devas. They supervise the development of species among all forms of water life, including the remarkable water-borne mammals. Working under an Aqui Angel, it is also the twans' responsibility to encourage and guide the evolutionary progress of all forms of water life under their influence.

A Seezal Blesses the Bluejay

In the same manner, two orders of devas serve the unfoldment of winged creatures ranging from insects to song birds to soaring condors. The first of these is the seezal order of devas, whose work is equivalent to the pentees. They are committed to the establishment of instinctive patterns among flying species, including migration habits. The second of these devic orders is composed of twilvee devas. Like their twan counterparts who serve sea life, the twilvee have charge of the evolutionary unfoldment of birds. Together, the seezal and twilvee devas perform a variety of vital services that support the evolution of winged creatures. As these groups advance, their destiny and that of all bird life is to enter the ranks of nature beings in the air realm, slowly progressing to devahood. Similarly, the water creatures unfold in their turn to devahood in the water realm. So it is that God's ongoing theme of growth and unfoldment is many-faceted and all-encompassing—a truth that offers humans an active role to play, if we have the wisdom and depth of caring to participate.

Humans as Animal Guides and Protectors

Like wild animals, those which have been domesticated also have Angel guides and protectors. However, animals that we have made part of our lives have an additional aid and server. Just as human beings rely on an older and more evolved Angel kingdom to safefold and guide us, so our domesticated animals look up to us for safekeeping and direction. The added blessing that humankind is privileged to give to the animals that we have made part of our lives is the opportunity to protect and guide them.

In a very real sense, we may show our appreciation of the Angel kingdom and begin to repay the enormous debt of service we owe to our Creator by the love and care we return to the animal kingdom. Flower herself urged all with whom she came in contact to have pets in their homes. Seeing how they blossom in confidence, intelligence, and love is a fitting reward that those taking part in the enterprise of caregiving can experience in no other way.

Moreover, the Aqui, Folatel, and Budiel Angels often turn to humans as the best available resource to protect, guide, and help animals gradually to ascend the ladder of evolution toward their own realization of individuality and service.

Consider, for example, the plight of a lost or abandoned dog. It is most likely frightened and bewildered. A Folatel Angel eager to help may often look to one of us for a solution. Perhaps out of the corner of our eye, we catch a glimpse of the forlorn creature glancing anxiously up and down the road. If we are responsive—and that is always the big "if" with humans—we will stop and befriend the animal.

When a human comes to the rescue of such an orphaned animal, the watching Folatel Angel's response is warm and immediate. Flower has described the sunburst of joy and thanksgiving that lights up the entire vicinity surrounding the suffering creature. She has said on many occasions that if we could ourselves witness the profound sense of gratitude which the Folatel Angel radiates when any human is the means of bringing aid and comfort to a creature for whom it is responsible, we would always go far out of our way in the future to render such service.

Questhaven Retreat, the center founded by Flower in 1940, is located out among chaparral-covered hills of southern California, miles from any city. The winding country road leading to the retreat is a favorite place for people to abandon unwanted pets. Over the years, Flower herself and many retreatants have picked up these castaways. After bathing them and nursing them back to health, the animals are often brought as guests to a Sunday service at the retreat where a visitor, moved by their plight and their charm, often adopts them. In this same spirit, pets are always welcome to attend services with their owners at the Church of the Holy Quest at Questhaven Retreat. Flower always put love for all creatures above traditional human attitudes to the contrary. Her vision allowed others to view openly an appreciation for animals. Often this awakened the entire congregation to a love for animals, even those people who previously had given little thought to the creatures' existence.

In her book *These, Too, Shall Be Loved*, Flower writes, "It has been said that just as man lifts his hand upward, that it may be clasped by a loving Angel, so must he extend his helpfulness downward to touch and influence for good the lives of the creatures. Striving to reach down and lift the lives of countless creatures has added new dimensions to my daily experiences. The friendships I have formed with these younger life forms have given me joys and blessings of a never-to-be-forgotten kind."

Once we are found to be responsive to the promptings of Folatel Angels, remarkable encounters often occur. Flower shared an experience she had in the years soon after founding Questhaven, when she was strongly drawn to cocker spaniels. She gathered books and articles on this breed and began visualizing one at her side. Then, on a lecture tour in Chicago, a member of the audience who was a breeder of cocker spaniels offered Flower one as a gift. For the next several years this lovable dog was her constant companion. Then one day the animal fell ill, and while the veterinarian was examining her, she died. Sadly, Flower returned to Questhaven, and there, standing at the entrance gate, was a cocker spaniel, obviously abandoned, who so closely resembled her dog that the two could have been litter mates. Scooping up the dog, Flower gave heartfelt thanks to its Folatel Angel for arranging such a timely gift.

A Loving Folatel Guides a Pet Home

Oftentimes, the helpfulness of a Folatel Angel protects an animal that has been frightened or lost. Flower tells of an incident involving a family's much loved cat. The family had taken the cat along on vacation in a mountain area where they owned a small cabin. When the family was preparing to return to their home, they stopped at the mountain landfill to dispose of some trash. In the brief moment that the car door was open, the cat jumped out and disappeared into the surrounding underbrush. The father, mother, and four children spread out to search, but an hour passed with no sign of the cat. It was nearing nightfall, and the possibility of having to go on without the cat was imminent. As a last resort, the family gathered together and prayed to the Folatel Angel of the region to guide them to their cat's hiding place. Within minutes, the mother was led to walk up the road into an open area some distance away, where the trees were sparse. One tree in particular attracted her attention. There, hiding in its uppermost branches, was the cat. With her heart singing in thanksgiving to the Folatel Angel, she was able to coax the cat down.

Then there was an occasion when Flower and her family were driving along a desert road on their way to a favorite mountain. All of a sudden, a very large Folatel Angel rose up into view some distance ahead. Flower was deeply moved to see this magnificent being, though it wasn't obvious what creature was being protected. The Angel signaled to Flower that a tiny dog was in need of a good home. A few moments later a small black puppy was seen trotting along the roadside. Obviously bedraggled and abandoned, the little female was quick to realize her good fortune and hopped in the car.

Flower took her home, named her Frolic, and enjoyed her company for the next fifteen years.

Setting emergencies aside, what the Folatel and Budiel Angels value most from humans is a daily cycle of attentive and loving care to the animals in their lives. The Angels would wish that we respect and cherish them, looking to their well-being with genuine concern and consistency. Taking them for daily walks, talking to them, giving them generous amounts of attention, and letting them know that they are valued members of our household all advance each animals' emerging personality and intelligence. When we sincerely render compassion for these younger forms of life, we are in the company of these citizens of heaven who rejoice to find humans constructively engaged with the creatures in their charge. Too often, what the Angels see is hunting and exploitation, abuse and neglect—hardly a basis for building the trust and harmony that enlightenment requires.

Angels and Animal Evolution

A single Aqui, Folatel, or Budiel Angel is responsible for hundreds of animals. The more advanced the Angel, the more expanded will be that being's circle of influence. Each Angel gradually evolves a preference for a particular line of animals. One, for example, might guide and support the animals passing through the sequence from jackal, coyote, fox, and wolf up to the dog. Similar sequences involving the lines of development characteristic of birds and fish likewise attract angelic sponsors.

Gradual advancement of animal forms from lower to higher stages of unfoldment is an underlying theme of all life on earth. The Angel presences mantling the world of creatures are deeply satisfied at the moments of transformation, when creatures under their care make an upward step, leaving outworn habits or fixed behaviors behind to advance into new capabilities.

Flower has taught that the universal nature of life is to ascend the ladder of evolution. It is this upward striving force that gives life its purpose and direction. Many humans are so wrapped up in their own preoccupations that they overlook this pattern, which humans share in common with all other living beings. Seeing how we humans can be of immense help, the Aqui, Folatel, and Budiel Angels patiently look forward to the dawning enlightenment that the Aquarian Age promises. Animals, after all, have rudimentary souls and a destiny that will one day bring them to their own line of mastery. We who constitute the human race have the opportunity, privilege, and obligation to band with the Angels to help all creatures toward their ultimate unfoldment.

A Cathedral in the Sanctuary of Nature

Chapter 8

 Finding Enlightenment through Nature

Our glimpse into the inner workings of the four realms of nature through the eyes of Flower's clairvoyance has widened our vision and increased our knowledge of what lies beyond the horizon of physical reality. This heightened awareness can make the inner worlds directly accessible. In this final chapter we turn to how this access can lay a foundation for finding in nature the beginnings of enlightenment.

Flower taught, and it is apparent to most of us, that nature is one of the most direct and powerful ways for us to experience God. In nature's cathedrals and wayside shrines, human seekers are received as welcomed worshipers. Those who have gone before us have spoken movingly of nature's sermons. American writer Maltbie D. Babcock observes in his *Thoughts from Everyday Living*:

This is my Father's world
And to my listening ears
All nature sings, and 'round me rings
The music of the spheres.

Charles Towne captures the same spirit in his *Selected Poems* (1925) when he writes:

I need not shout my faith. Thrice eloquent
Are quiet trees and green listening sod:
Hushed are the stars, whose power is never spent.
The hills are mute: yet how they speak of God.

Preparing for a Sojourn into Nature

How can we prepare ourselves in a practical way to make a trip into nature an opportunity for spiritual advancement? To open our minds to such thoughts, we must be more than creatures of worldly preoccupation and become as well fit vessels of receptivity to God's wisdom and creativity. If this is our goal, the first step is purification, clearing our minds of clutter and debris. Ideally, this cleansing should take place a week in advance of entering a temple of nature, such as a national park or mountain region. Our preparation can include reading the works of naturalists and nature mystics who have found profound spiritual truths in nature's holy places. Look for those writers who are not only factual about what they see, but who glimpse the handiwork of the Creator in the natural wonders they write about. John Muir, author of *The Mountains of California,* has already been mentioned as a suitable source. Other writers whose works express this perspective are Edwin Way Teale *(Circle of the Seasons),* Hal Borland *(Our Natural World),* Edwin Bernbaum *(Sacred Mountains of the World),* Henry Beston *(The Outermost House),* Sigurd Olson *(Listening Point),* and Henry David Thoreau *(Walden).*

Another helpful form of preparation is visualization. When we sit in meditation, we can visualize the inner side of nature, the beings and intelligences, such as those described in these pages, that we might well encounter on our journey. We can also visualize good weather conditions, safe travel, and comfortable accommodations—all the practical considerations that make our journey into nature free of distractions. At the same time, it is important for us to visualize ourselves meeting any inconveniences or trials constructively, so that we are not caught off guard, if unforeseen circumstances do arise.

Helpful in our planning excursions into nature are Flower's comments on the degree of receptivity one might expect from beings representing the four realms of nature. Earth and air beings are most inclined to give individual attention to humans. Conditions for this favorable reception are at their best in mountains, where the devas are the freest to attend to our particular needs, provided we present ourselves unselfishly. Earth beings are admirers of selflessness and are repelled by persons who have self-serving motives. Air beings, in their turn, are admirers of loyalty—to family, to one's goals, and especially to spiritual ideals. Water beings are least concerned with humans, though the one human quality they most admire is emotional stability. Fire beings have little interest in humans until they reach angelhood. The quality they admire most is purity. As noted, the Angels of Fire fan the flames of holy enthusiasm and spiritual ardor.

A final and vital act of our preparation, one that is the hallmark of any spiritual quest, is to become self-emptied and God-filled. To whatever degree we are able to achieve it, a twin sense of humility and wonder fine tunes our faculties for inner perception—namely, receptivity to intuitions, impressions and, ultimately, the presence of God. We should keep in mind what we have gleaned from earlier chapters about how nature beings are repelled by any signs of self-centeredness. To avoid such an inhibiting state of mind, we can steep ourselves in the wonder of God's creation until we feel ourselves dissolving like a dewdrop in the sea of God's immensity. More than a fanciful analogy, this metaphor expresses the essence of life's most transcendent experience, one with the power to transport us into other dimensions of consciousness.

An Elf in the Garden

Flower further advises that we embark on any pilgrimage into nature in the promising mood of holy expectancy. If one goes on a spiritual quest fully anticipating insights, discoveries, and revelations, this all-encompassing viewpoint can transform not only how we experience nature but how we see people and events along the way. It allows our perceptions to transcend what otherwise might be ordinary and commonplace experiences, revealing that God exists in everyone and everything. Such a state of mind makes our days into a life-changing adventure and makes us fit students for the instructors awaiting us in the school of nature.

One immediate result of a mood of holy expectancy is enriched perceptiveness, the capacity to see more deeply into divine reality. This enrichment involves not only the traditional five senses, but the sixth sense as well. The great gift of nature

is that it offers a feast for the senses. As we walk along nature's pathways, we may see trees and flowers as if for the first time. As we listen to the soft, sighing wind in a grove of lofty pines or the lyrical melody of a joyful mountain brook, we hear hymns of praise sung to the Supreme Presence. Nor are the other senses overlooked. There is a tangy sweetness to the fruitfulness of nature that we can savor. With this tasting comes the fresh scents of a thousand fragrances riding on a sea wind or an alpine breeze and shifting with the seasons. One's sense of touch is stirred by embracing the trunk of a grand old tree or by feeling a grassy meadow against our bodies as we pause to rest and review the gleanings of our journey thus far.

We are immersed in a celebration of our most refined senses when we venture out into nature's temples. Yet there remains the mysterious sixth sense, which transcends the sum of the other five. It is the one that Flower called upon to experience the inner realms of nature. For most of us, it has its beginnings in intuition and impressions, the sensing of insights and realities that come to us from our inner knowing. Often these openings appear to us in the form of a sudden realization or recognition. While the source of these illuminating experiences is usually veiled, we might surmise that the Angel kingdom is one of its most frequent contributors. This realization is especially true when we are alone in nature, reverently attuned to the energies and rhythms of this dimension.

When we visit the wilderness, it is time to walk at a slow pace, taking in the stream of observations and thoughts that quietly, luminously come to our attention. Our minds should be like finely tuned instruments, immersed in a worshipful awareness of peace and God's presence. A mood of holy expectancy prompts us to look forward to little revelations that come to us as the gifts of a deepening awareness. At its heart lies the art of seeing "a world in a grain of sand," as the poet Blake expressed it. And, we ask ourselves, have we really looked at the grains of sand that lie scattered through our lives, which we dismissed as the commonest among the common-place? Holy expectancy brings us to the magical moment when we cross the threshold of perception to see worlds within worlds. The essence of this state of mind is that it is the observer, not the observed, which is transformed.

Ascending a Mountain Trail

There is no better setting for an experience of natural transcendence than a mountain trail. As we ascend, our thoughts can turn to insights from our readings of naturalists who revere the Creator of all. As John Muir said, "The clearest way into the universe is through a forest wilderness." What an invocation for anyone receptive to its invitation. Like George

MacDonald, nineteenth-century Scottish mystic and writer, we can open ourselves to the belief that "every fact of nature is a revelation of God." Awakening our souls with such an attitude insures that we will not miss any discovery along our way. It also makes our trip into nature a spiritual quest, a high adventure whose possibilities are unlimited.

To receive the keenest inspiration, it is helpful for us to choose a trail that is new to us. Walking with an inner feeling of anticipation of the holy, we should continually reaffirm our purpose on the path, saying frequently to God, "I desire to find Thee, everywhere." Again and again, we return our thoughts to our longing to discover more of divinity in the wilderness of nature.

Among the lessons nature provides, one which may seem contrary to the enthusiasm with which we often begin our journeys, is patience. It is a natural human tendency to expect instant revelations, when what God really expects of us is transformation. It is a familiar spiritual law that in order to receive, we must give, and giving often consists of getting ourselves out of the way so that we can see that which lies beyond ourselves. Thus it is that every walk in nature may not find us at a point of readiness to receive fresh insights. Our response to this should not be disappointment, but persever-ance and trust. Nature is so pristine that we humans are often not fit to share in its secrets.

An Inquisitive Gnome

When we remember that it is our responsibility to be properly prepared and receptive, we will be clear about where our focus belongs.

As our journey unfolds, we can ask questions of the nature presences surrounding us. For example, what is the one lesson this moment finds me ready to realize? Or, does the spirit of this forest have a particular keynote or theme? As these and other questions are posed, we might usefully see ourselves as pupils in the early grades of an ageless school and keep in mind that, crucial to our learning, is our openness and our humility before the wisdom that nature so abundantly expresses.

As we ascend what has now become a spiritual path, our thoughts reflecting our deep love for God's wonder-filled creation, we can begin to study the most revealing of all arts leading to enlightenment in nature, the language of signs and symbols. God's handwriting can be seen in trees, rocks, gnarled pieces of wood, and other message-laden natural objects. Flower never tired of the pleasure such instruction gave her. The remarkable secret to this mystic way of communication with the world of nature is not to focus on it directly and deliberately, but simply to be receptive while our minds are filled with wonder and appreciation. Then nature's treasures speak volumes.

Some natural symbols are encoded in a universal language: a fragment of wood shaped like an upward twist tapering off to a point signifies the flame of aspiration; a triangular stone indicates the ascent up the mountain of God; a section of bark surrounding an open knothole suggests the single eye of illumination, and so on. Other symbols have a more personal message. Flower tells of the time when she found a small piece of wood about the size of a child's palm. One side was ghoulish looking and forbidding, but the other side suggested a cameo figure of a Madonna. When she discovered this object, Flower had been praying for a man who was maladjusted and whose background was very earthy and prodigal. To her, the ghoulish side of the piece of wood was the forbidding side of this man's personality, but the tiny portrait of the Madonna on the reverse suggested that he had a dual nature and that his gentler, finer character was beginning to emerge.

Flower also tells of finding objects of stone and wood lying in her path which resembled blue birds, owls, dogs, squirrels, elves, hearts and, once, a gazelle's head, deftly sculptured as if fashioned by a woodcarver. Each had its own pertinent and revealing messages. She adds the further observation that her best finds have always been near at hand, as if disclosed and highlighted for her particular notice.

Another of Flower's gleanings from years of seeking God in nature is the awareness that our sixth sense does not stir until we are deeply in love with all that we see. When we awaken to a profound spiritual love for all that nature contains, every faculty we possess rejoices. Crossing this threshold, at last we see and sense that which we had only intimations of previously. Some individuals can get no farther than an awareness of their entire being sensing God. Should we be able to achieve even this much recognition, we are touching the boundaries of cosmic consciousness. With this attainment, we experience an outpouring of joy unlike anything previously known—a joyousness that comes from touching the fringes of enlightenment.

Although we may wish direct contact with the Infinite Spirit, until our sixth sense is fully functioning, it is wise for us to exercise creatively our five physical senses until they give some indication of the immanence of God. In the mountains even our sense of smell becomes sharper and more pleasurable. As we strive to rediscover divinity in our surroundings, we become conscious of faint inklings of things present but invisible. Our intuitional antennas locate currents of luminous energy flowing into the region we are exploring.

As we reach the summit of our ascent, we may sense from which one of several nearby mountain peaks the refreshing baptism flows. We intuit a presence in its heights that is unusually vital, which touches us in ways that cause our spirits to soar. In its wake, every atom of our being is stimulated and invigorated.

On our several rests in descending the trail, we may choose to sit with our back against a sturdy pine, or we may lie flat on the ground with our eyes opened to the sky overhead. Studying the silvery tips of the surrounding evergreens, we notice the release of etheric energy streaming gently heaven-ward, a rite of cleansing and restoration. We can use this time to practice our own form of release. Into the boundless canopy of blue sky, we can release our uncertainties, our insecurities, and our reluctance to return to routine duties and events. We can take comfort that the transforming power of our pilgrimage will remain fresh and alive within us and will remain with us into eternity.

As we descend farther down the mountain trail, our thoughts savor the rich harvest of experience that the day has brought us. Often we were in the presence of tree devas, and our knowledge of their vibrant reality brought us closer to the individual trees over which they watch. How much more appreciative we are now of these stalwart forest sentinels! When we felt the brisk wind currents coursing through the stands of pines higher up the mountain slope, we remembered the Murmlo, Angels of the air realm, who fashion the rivers of wind that bathe the planet. Listening with ears open to the Divine, we heard them sing a soft, sighing symphony of praise to the Creator.

As the shadows of the approaching evening lengthen, sunset colors fill the sky and paint the landscape, reminding us of the artistry of the Angels of Morning and Evening who so magnificently begin and conclude the day. And as the sunset lights the western horizon, we settle on a rocky ledge from which to witness the gathering glory. It is the hour for reflection, assimilation, and reconsecration. Much has been learned in the classroom of nature in the last hours. Most of all, we have realized the essential importance of appreciation of nature in the quest for enlightenment. More than interest or attention, appreciation of the kind Flower describes amounts to falling in love with nature and all that contains. Such love takes us beyond the surface of creation into the heart of each sight, each sound, each sensation. What was previously an ordinary flower, seen through new eyes, becomes a masterpiece of beauty and revelation. Each delicate blossom enfolds the secrets of the universe.

Appreciation of nature's inner beauty leads to insight, the fountainhead of enlightenment. A sympathetic and perceptive insight into nature can lead us out of the jungle of worldly preoccupation onto the alpine meadows on the slopes of God's mountain. It was Flower's keen perception that most distinguished her from other seers and teachers. Nothing that her gaze fell on was ordinary. Because she was transformed, the world around her was transformed. That was her gift to those who knew her.

Journals and Other Tools of Insight

Anyone seeking enlightenment through nature will find a journal to be a valuable tool. A journal can be a record of our adventures and discoveries, along with their accompanying trials and challenges, and also measure our progress. As a record, a journal allows us to recapture the highlights of various journeys, especially those that were instructive or illuminating. While each journey is distinctive, looked at together, they often disclose a pattern, much like a trail which winds back and forth as it ascends to a mountain summit. The sequence of discoveries often suggests an intriguing story line that is, in retrospect, remarkable and appropriate. From this sequence emerges a pattern that is both personally illuminating and sheds light on the psychology of enlightenment.

Sometimes it is not the pattern but a single instance which is so luminous with revelation that it becomes archetypal. Flower tells of one such experience. She was in the midst of preparing a new series of lessons for an upcoming program. To relieve the pressure of her time-consuming task, she went to her favorite mountain retreat. But still the weight of deadlines clung to her. In the morning she took up her journal and said to herself, "I've had enough! I do not need to live with a consciousness oppressed by too many things to do. I can be free!" She then set out to walk on a mountain trail. But even her ardent prayers and the freshness of the scene were not enough to ease her mind.

She came at last to a tree that she loved. Leaning against it, she looked up and breathed one deeper prayer, "There must be freedom, release, and peace. Teach me!" At that moment a wonderful presence she recognized as her Guardian Angel, spoke to her, "Look up and be impressed by what you see." Obeying this request, Flower looked up into the beautiful azure sky with scattered clumps of white clouds moving across the blue expanse in freedom, order, and the ecstasy of serenity. There was no hurry. There was no pressure. There was only an immensity that was purifying. It rinsed her free of the day's burdens and restored her peace and freedom.

She didn't keep track of how long she stood watching the vaulted heavens, but suddenly her mind began to receive instruction from her soul about the empowerment of the immensity of consciousness itself. Like opening a flood gate, the themes of the lessons she needed to prepare poured out into the pages of her journal. For Flower it was a life-changing experience.

This kind of discovery awaits us all in nature. We, too, can find in it restoration, revelation, and transformation. The wilderness can soothe our pains, heal our wounds, redress our mistakes, open our eyes, brighten our outlook, engage our hearts, illumine our minds. Immersion in nature helps us move beyond ourselves and cross the threshold of God awareness. The secret password to this crossing is love of God and all creation. It is the credo by which Flower lived her life.

Flower summed up this truth clearly, offering the practical advice of one for whom nature and its Angels had been the kindest and most illuminating instructors: "Nature can be the greatest teacher of our souls this side of Christ. Prepare yourself for encounters with nature by being quiet and listening with keen perceptiveness. You need to walk alone to behold, to think, to feel, to be instructed. Be reverent, be appreciative, be perceptive. Watch the horizons. All of a sudden, everything will change, and you will find yourself stilled in wonder. You will be so at one with the intelligence of nature that from your encounter will come a shower of inflowing power, the like of which you have never before received. As you walk farther, you will find yourself analyzing what has been shown you. It is a benediction from those presences which are always watching wherever one goes in nature's realms. Keep your mind open and inquiring as you walk, ever improving control of your will, your receptivity, your teachableness, your sense of wonder. Be God-filled, God-hungry, and God-enlightened."

When we follow this sage advice, the Angels of nature will certainly flock to our aid. With their help, and with the glory of nature as our classroom and our cathedral, we can, as Shakespeare put it,

> *Find tongues in trees, books in running brooks,*
> *Sermons in stones, and good in everything.*

Glossary

Air Realm	The branch of the nature kingdom concerned with beings caring for the planet's atmosphere and well-being.
Airwee (AIR wee)	Advanced Angels of the air realm supervising the atmosphere and weather.
Allrays (ALL rays)	The youngest Angels in the earth realm, also known as Angels of the Heights.
Allsees (ALL sees)	Advanced Angels serving the earth realm. They reside in mountain regions throughout the planet and are responsible for vast areas.
Amfri (AHM free)	Youngest of the Angels in the fire realm whose work is to inspire humans toward enlightenment.
Angel Kingdom	The great line of evolution complementing its human counterpart which encompasses the four waves serving the Lord Christ, the Holy Spirit, Life Motivation, and Nature.
Angel of the Christ Presence	A highly advanced Angel, usually of Archangel rank, who serves in the Divine Love Wave under the Lord Christ.

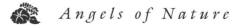

Angels of the Evening	Angels of the fire realm who create sunsets and dispense frequencies of rest and reflection.
Angels of the Morning	Angels of the fire realm who create sunrises and dispense energies of awakening and reconsecration.
Angel Prince	A title given to the supreme Tija in charge of the earth's atmosphere or water.
Aqui (AH kwee)	Advanced Angels serving the animal kingdom whose work is to prepare animals for higher stages of advancement.
Budiel (BOOD ee el)	Angels serving the animal kingdom whose work is to guide the progress and growth of animal's individual characteristics.
Builders	The youngest and smallest elementals in the air realm who facilitate the exchange of carbon dioxide for oxygen.
Cilarae (kih LAIR eye)	The youngest Angels of the air realm, also known as Angels of Winds. Their work is managing the air currents caused by the earth's rotation.
Clairvoyant	One who can see into the higher dimensions, including auras, thought forms, nature beings, and Angels.

Glossary

Deva (DAY vah)	An advanced nature being standing one rank below angelhood.
Divine Love Wave	One of four waves of angelic activity serving the planet and involved with the Lord Christ and the unfoldment of love.
Divine Wisdom Wave	One of four waves of angelic activity serving our planet and involved with the Holy Spirit and the unfoldment of wisdom.
Earth realm	The branch of the nature kingdom concerned with beings caring for the earth and its botanical life.
Electric Angels	Angels of the air realm who deal with magnetism and forces of electricity.
Elemental	The youngest form of nature beings serving each of the four realms of nature.
Elves	Nature beings in the earth realm one rank above elementals. Their responsibility is caring for the larger plants and shrubs.
Fairies	A common name for earth elementals otherwise known as frakins.
Fire realm	The branch of the nature kingdom concerned with beings caring for the element of fire and its function.

Firl (furl)	Advanced Angels of the fire realm whose work is to take humans through the gateways of initiation and illumination.
Flamin (FLAH min)	Nature beings of the fire realm who have reached devahood.
Folatel (fo LAY tel)	Angels serving the animal kingdom whose work is caring for their physical well-being and safety.
Frakins (FRAH kin)	Nature beings in the earth realm that are at the final stage of unfoldment as elementals. They are commonly called fairies.
Gnomes	Nature beings in the earth realm one rank above elves. They are caretakers particularly of the soil and minerals.
Guardians of the Threshold	Angels of the air realm responsible for the upbringing and training of the zephyrs.
Initiatory Angel	A special designation for an Angel who presides at the advancement of another Angel or nature being who is evolving through a series of initiatory thresholds.
Life Motivation Wave	One of four waves of angelic activity serving our planet and involved with karma and human evolution.

Glossary

Lords of the Mountains — Great beings of advanced Angel rank who preside over spiritually charged mountain citadels. They impart the keynote qualities for an entire mountain region.

Murmlo (MURM lo) — Angels of the air realm who influence storms and changes in the weather.

Mystic — One who has direct communication with God and the Inner Worlds.

Naiads (NY add) — Nature beings in the water realm who have attained devahood, whose work is to preserve the destiny of rivers.

Nature being — A general term for the inner life supporting the four realms of nature and including all those below the rank of angelhood.

Nature Wave — One of four waves of angelic activity serving our planet and involved with the world of nature.

Neentel (NEEN tel) — Angels of the air realm who work with the Murmlo to influence seasonal weather patterns.

Nereids (NEAR ee ids) — Angels of the water realm who help supervise the destiny of rivers, lakes, and oceans.

Oceanids
(OH shun ids)
The youngest elemental forms in the water realm who purify and energize units of water.

Pentee
(pen TEE)
Devas serving the animal kingdom who regulate the fixed habits and cyclic experiences of fish.

Petris
(PEET riz)
Highly advanced Angels in the fire realm whose work is interplanetary in nature.

River Kings
Advanced devas of the water realm who govern the rivers of the world.

Salamanders
Nature beings of the fire realm one rank above fire elementals.

Sea Lords
Unusually advanced Angels of the water realm who are in charge of oceans and the larger rivers and lakes.

Sea nymphs
Nature beings of the water realm who guide the currents of moving bodies of water.

Seezal
(see ZAL)
Devas serving the animal kingdom who establish instinctive patterns among birds.

Solar Logos
The Supreme Godhead of our solar system.

Sylphs
Nature beings of the air realm who are advanced devas. They work to control air currents and protect the earth from harmful cosmic rays.

Glossary

Tija
(TEE jah)

The highest and most exalted of air or water intelligences, mostly of Archangel rank or higher, dwelling in the stratosphere.

Tree devas

Nature beings of the earth realm one rank below angelhood, who are responsible for the well-being of trees and forests.

Twan
(twahn)

Devas serving the animal kingdom who encourage the evolutionary progress of all forms of water life.

Twilvee
(TWIL vee)

Devas serving the animal kingdom who assist the evolutionary unfoldment of birds.

Water realm

The branch of the nature kingdom concerned with beings caring for the planet's water resources and cycles.

Water sprites

Nature beings of the water realm one rank above the oceanids whose function is to facilitate the exchange of water to vapor.

Zephyrs
(ze furs)

Nature beings of the air realm who are at the first stage of devahood. Their work is to guide the air currents.

Index

Index

Angels of Nature

New Zealand, 43, 50
   tree devas in, 43
Newhouse, Lawrence, x
Nirvana, 2

—O—

Ocean Lord, 81
oceanids, 74
Odyssey, 73
Old Testament, 2
Olson, Sigurd, 115
Olympus, 2

—P—

Pacific Northwest, 35
Pacific Ocean, 80
Paradise, 2
pentee devas, 103
Pericos, 80
Petris, 99
Poseidon, 81
Powers, 5
Principalities, 5
Psalms, 2

—Q—

Questhaven Retreat, x, 99, 107

—R—

Realm of Fire, 87
Realm of the Air, 55

Realm of the Earth, 31
Realm of Water, 73
Rediscovering the Angels, xi
redwoods, 23, 32
release of divine wisdom, 6
Revelation, 2

—S—

salamanders, 89
Sea Lord, 80
sea nymphs, 73, 76
seezal devas, 104
sequoias, 23, 32
Seraphim, 5
Shakespeare, 129
Shinto, v
Sirens, 73
Snoqualmie Falls, 78
Solar
   Angels, 95
   Logos, 96
southern California, 35
Spirit of the Redwoods, 44
spiritual
   aspiration, 90
   evolution, 91
Switzerland, 50
sylphs, 57, 62

—T—

Teal, Edwin Way, 18, 115
These, Too, Shall Be Loved, 107
Thoreau, Henry David, 18, 115

QUEST BOOKS
are published by
the Theosophical Society in America
Wheaton, Illinois 60189–0270,
a branch of a world organization
dedicated to the promotion of the unity of
humanity and the encouragement of the study of
religion, philosophy, and science, to the end that
we may better understand ourselves and our place in
the universe. The Society stands for complete
freedom of individual search and belief.
In the Classics Series well-known
theosophical works are made
available in popular editions.